Moses Harvey

Newfoundland in 1897

Being Queen Victoria's Diamond Jubilee Year and the Four Hundredth Anniversary

of the Discovery of the Island by John Cabot

Moses Harvey

Newfoundland in 1897

Being Queen Victoria's Diamond Jubilee Year and the Four Hundredth Anniversary of the Discovery of the Island by John Cabot

ISBN/EAN: 9783337059507

Printed in Europe, USA, Canada, Australia, Japan

Cover: Foto ©ninafisch / pixelio.de

More available books at **www.hansebooks.com**

NEWFOUNDLAND

IN

1897

BEING

QUEEN VICTORIA'S DIAMOND JUBILEE YEAR

AND

THE FOUR HUNDREDTH ANNIVERSARY OF THE DISCOVERY OF THE ISLAND BY JOHN CABOT

BY THE

REV. M. HARVEY, LL.D., F.R.S.C.

AUTHOR OF

"TEXT-BOOK OF NEWFOUNDLAND HISTORY;" ARTICLES "NEWFOUNDLAND," "LABRADOR," AND "SEAL FISHERIES OF THE WORLD," IN THE "ENCYCLOPÆDIA BRITANNICA;" "LECTURES LITERARY AND BIOGRAPHICAL;" "HANDBOOK AND TOURIST'S GUIDE OF NEWFOUNDLAND;" AND ONE OF THE AUTHORS OF "NEWFOUNDLAND: THE OLDEST BRITISH COLONY"

WITH MAP AND ILLUSTRATIONS

LONDON
SAMPSON LOW, MARSTON & COMPANY
LIMITED
St. Dunstan's House
FETTER LANE, FLEET STREET, E.C.
1897

PREFACE.

IN the following pages I have endeavoured to present, in a small compass, a comprehensive and accurate account of Newfoundland—England's first Colony—as it is in this year which witnesses the celebration of Her Majesty Queen Victoria's Diamond Jubilee.

Her auspicious reign of sixty years has been especially marked by the expansion and progress of the Colonial portion of her dominions. It may be truly affirmed that with her accession to the throne began that enlightened policy, on the part of the mother-country, under which the Colonies have made such a marvellous advance in population, wealth, and importance. Not only so, but these Colonies, as they have been filling up with an English-speaking people, have been gradually drawing closer, all these years, in intercourse, in feeling, in sincere attachment, to the mother of them all. The ties that bind them together have been multiplying and strengthening. The causes that once led to alienation and discord have disappeared and passed into oblivion.

Thus it has come to pass that in this Jubilee Year a strong desire for closer union discovers itself unmistakably. If the Colonial children have been growing in affection, it is not less true that England has also been moving nearer to them in parental feeling and thought; and now from both of them comes the cry, "We are one."

The illustrious reign of our beloved Queen may, and I trust will, be rendered still more glorious by the initiation of a movement towards the grand consummation of the Federation of the Colonies with the mother-land; by which they may become integral parts of one great whole, linked by ties that coming years will render stronger and stronger.

In this year, when the Colonies will be worthily represented in the pomp and pageantry which the great celebration calls for, and when, doubtless, they will be much in men's thoughts and in their speech, it seems not inopportune to present some account of England's first Colony, of which so little is known, but in which the feeling of .loyal attachment to the throne and empire is, and has ever been, true and strong.

The story of Newfoundland, in many ways, is one of unique interest. Here England achieved her first success in maritime discovery. Here her first attempt at planting a Colony was made. In prosecuting the fisheries of Newfoundland, English sailors first learned how to rule the waves. The wealth derived from these fisheries helped largely to build up England's commercial greatness. For many years its fisheries were the best nursery for her seamen; and they ultimately

PREFACE. vii

led to the founding of English Colonies for their protection and prosecution. Great and heroic men took part in the early colonization of the island, and the glory which their names shed on its history should never be forgotten. A knowledge of the changes, struggles, and sufferings through which its people passed can never fail to be one of deep interest.

I have devoted the main portion of this volume to a description of the natural resources and capabilities of the island. These have been largely overlooked, or misrepresented, and, as a consequence, undervalued and neglected. The account given in these pages of the agricultural and mineral resources of the country, and of its forest wealth, will be a surprise to many. I have endeavoured, however, in dealing with the subject, to secure strict accuracy of statement, and to be guided solely by facts, and by the best authorities. These natural resources, as I believe, and as ascertained facts prove, are very great, and such as warrant us in predicting a bright and prosperous future for the Colony, now that the construction of railways has opened its agricultural, mineral, and forest lands, and prepared a way for enterprise and capital to turn them to profitable account. I have also dwelt at some length on the fisheries—the grand staple industry of the Colony. Other topics are dealt with, especially the condition of the finances, trade, education, Government, the railways, public institutions, and the characteristics of the people. The scenery, climate, sporting capabilities, have not been overlooked. The improvements of the last twenty-five years are also pointed out, as well as the coming improvements, which may be fairly regarded as potentially included in these.

This Jubilee Year is also rendered memorable by the celebration of the four hundredth anniversary of the discovery of North America, and with it that of Newfoundland. I have, therefore, given some prominence to Cabot's great achievement, so pregnant with great results.

A residence of forty-five years in the Colony has given me opportunities of becoming acquainted with the country and the people. It will be a source of gratification to me if this little volume should aid in making the country better known, and attracting to it that attention which it richly merits.

M. HARVEY.

St. John's, Newfoundland,
   May, 1897.

CONTENTS.

CHAPTER I.

Discovery of North America by John Cabot—Voyage of the *Matthew* 1

CHAPTER II.

A Missing Chapter in History — Cabot's Reward — Meagre Records of his Voyage—The Landfall—Difficulty of determining it—Competing Theories—Cabot's Second Voyage, 1498—Historical Injustice to Sebastian Cabot—Estimate of his Character and Work—Cabot the Discoverer of Newfoundland—Object of the Fourth Centenary Celebration ... 12

CHAPTER III.

Reverence for our Noble Dead—Union of England's Ocean-Empire—Her Need of her Colonies—Homes for an Increasing Population—Mistakes of the Past in dealing with the Colonies—Beginnings in Newfoundland—The Fishing Era—Bretons and Basques First—The English follow—Expansion of English Fishing at Newfoundland—Genesis of Settlement—Value of Fisheries—Results—Sir Humphrey Gilbert takes Possession of the Island—His Heroic Death—Loss to Newfoundland—Queen Elizabeth and Queen Victoria—The Colonies in Victoria's Reign—Free Institutions ... 34

CONTENTS.

CHAPTER IV.

The Makers and Making of Newfoundland—Abortive Attempts at Colonizing—The Fishermen the Real Colonizers—Monopoly of West-Country Adventurers—Its Growth and Extent—Tyranny by Act of Parliament—The Fishing Admirals—Struggles of the Resident Population for Freedom—Dawn after Darkness—First Governor—Liberty slowly won against Heavy Odds—Wrongs of the Colony—Progress of Newfoundland in the Reign of Queen Victoria 56

CHAPTER V.

Evolution of the Railway in Newfoundland—Pioneer Roadmaking Seventy Years ago—Inception of a Railway—Sir William Whiteway, the Railway Leader—Opposition to the Project—Story of the Construction of the Great Northern and Western Railway—R. G. Reid, Esq, Contractor—Resources of the Country opened up—Character of the Contract—Advantages to the Colony—Settlement on Lands—Forests and Mineral Riches—Will the Railway be remunerative? 77

CHAPTER VI.

Development of Mining in Newfoundland—First Copper Mine: how discovered—Predictions of Science—Value of Copper Export—Increasing Demand for Copper—Iron Pyrites—Pilley's Island—Belle Isle Iron Mine; Enormous Deposit—Asbestos Mining—Discovery of Gold-bearing Quartz—Lead and Silver Ores—Petroleum on the West Coast ... 89

CHAPTER VII.

Newfoundland as an Agricultural and Lumbering Country—Extent of Arable and Grazing Land—Value of Farm Products and Domestic Animals—Liberality of Land Acts—Homestead Acts—Paper Pulp Act—Forest Wealth—The Climate 104

CONTENTS. xi

CHAPTER VIII.

Fisheries the Stable Industry of the People—Their Value—Arctic Current essential to Fish-life—Food of the Cod—Annual Catch of Cod—Fisheries Department—Stability of the Fisheries—Seal Fishery—Its Value—Mode of pursuing it—Herring Fishery—Salmon and Lobster Fisheries—Improvements needed 112

CHAPTER IX.

Form of Government—Evolution of Self-government—How the Colony is governed—Vote by Ballot—Manhood Suffrage—Working of Responsible Government—Education called for as a Safeguard—Judicature—Constabulary—Fire Department—Post Office 124

CHAPTER X.

Newfoundland's Revenue—Rate of Taxation—Public Debt per Head: how represented—State of the Revenue at Present—Retrenchment Policy—Late Commercial Crisis: Rapid recovery from—Financial Condition at the Close of 1896—Reforms 136

CHAPTER XI.

Scenery of the Island: the Norway of the New World—Health Resort: the Summers—Attractions for Travellers and Tourists—Novelty of the Scenery—The Fishermen—Professors Bickmore and Hyatt on the Character of the Scenery and Climate—Captain Kennedy's Testimony—Archbishop of Halifax: his Experience—The London *Times* on Newfoundland—Sport and Angling—Grouse-shooting—Deer-stalking 144

CHAPTER XII.

Geographical Position of the Island—Its Importance—Bays—Coast-line—Population—Saxon and Celtic Elements—Education: Schools, Colleges, Scholarships—Higher Education—Educational Grant—Religious Denominations Social aspects—Condition of the People 156

CHAPTER XIII.

Influence of the New World on the Old—Great Duel between England and France for Supremacy in North America—Its Bearing on Newfoundland—Treaty of Utrecht—The Beginning of Troubles—Evils of Concessions to the French—Misinterpretation of the Treaties—Their Injury to the Colony—Lobster Difficulty on the Treaty Shore—Delegation to the House of Lords—Best Policy for the Colony ... 163

APPENDIX I.—The Great Seal-Hunt of Newfoundland ... 173

„ II.—Notes on Chapter II.—Sebastian Cabot ... 189

„ III.—Cabot Commemoration 193

„ IV.—The Mission to Deep-Sea Fishermen ... 194

INDEX 195

LIST OF ILLUSTRATIONS.

	PAGE
SIR WILLIAM V. WHITEWAY ...	*Frontispiece*
LADY WHITEWAY ...	*Frontispiece*
ICEBERG	*To face* 32
STEADY BROOK FALLS	,, 48
RATTLING BROOK, EXPLOITS RIVER ...	,, 64
TOAD'S COVE	,, 80
PLACENTIA RAILWAY STATION	,, 90
NEW IRON-MINE, BELLE ISLE: APPARATUS FOR SHIPPING ORE	,, 96
FISH-MAKING IN THE NARROWS OF ST. JOHN'S	,, 112
SEALING STEAMER LOADED, AND ENTERING ST. JOHN'S HARBOUR	,, 118
PETTY HARBOUR, SOUTH OF ST. JOHN'S	,, 128
THE NARROWS AND HARBOUR OF ST. JOHN'S	,, 136
SHELL BIRD ISLAND, HUMBER RIVER	,, 144
HUMBER RIVER (NEAR ENTRANCE)	,, 152
DEVIL'S DANCING POINT, HUMBER RIVER	,, 160
THE DUNGEON, BONAVISTA ... ... ,	168
PANNING SEALS	173
PUTTING SEALS ON BOARD	176

LIST OF ILLUSTRATIONS.

	PAGE
SCALPING THE SEALS	177
WHITE-COAT SEAL	180
S.S. "NEPTUNE" IN THE ICE	182
HAULING THE PELTS	184
THREE CANADIAN BANKERS ON THE ICE OF ST. JOHN'S, CONTEMPLATING A YOUNG SEAL FROM A FINANCIAL STANDPOINT	187
FULL-GROWN HARP SEAL	188

MAP.

NEWFOUNDLAND ... ... *To face* 1

NEWFOUNDLAND:
ENGLAND'S OLDEST COLONY.
By Rev. M. HARVEY, LL.D.

London: Sampson Low, Marston & Co., Ld.

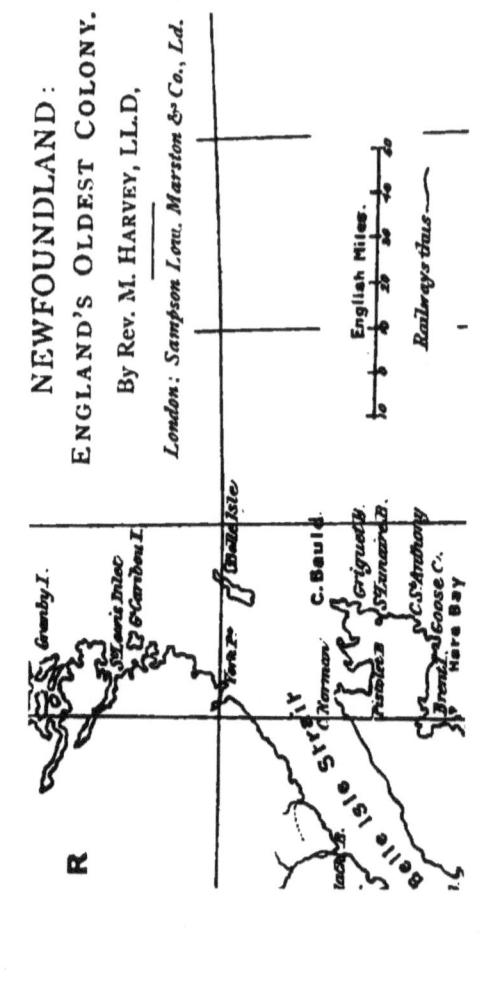

NEWFOUNDLAND:
ENGLAND'S OLDEST COLONY.

CHAPTER I.

Discovery of North America by John Cabot—Voyage of the
Matthew.

FOUR hundred years ago, on the 2nd of May, 1497, a little vessel of some sixty tons burthen took her departure from the port of Bristol and turned her prow towards the stormy unknown wastes of the North Atlantic. On her stern she bore the name, "The *Matthew*, of Bristol." Her commander was John Cabot, a Venetian by birth, but for some time resident in Bristol. He had obtained a patent from Henry VII. of England for the discovery of new lands to the westward, and with a crew of eighteen stout West-Country sailors, he now embarked on his perilous enterprise.

The expedition attracted little or no attention. In silence, without any pomp or circumstance, the little craft spread her sails on this bright May morning, and dropped down Bristol Channel, unnoticed among the other tiny vessels that then furrowed its waters. But there were daring spirits on board from the West Country, the country noted long afterwards for its warriors, statesmen, discoverers—its Raleighs, Davises, Gilberts, Grenvilles, Drakes, Hawkinses—of some whom, not without reason, the great Elizabeth said, "The men of Devon are my right hand." We do not know the name of a single officer or sailor on board the *Matthew;* and even of her brave commander, John Cabot, we know very little. We must judge these daring navigators by their deeds, for perhaps never was there an enterprise having such far-reaching consequences and exerting such an influence on the destinies of humanity, of which so little notice was taken at the time, and so few and meagre records have been preserved. So far as known, no diary was kept on board the *Matthew*, and her commander gave to the world but little account of what took place beyond the bare results of the voyage. The voyage of Columbus has thrown around it the glamour of poetry and romance. History has gathered into her golden urn every incident connected with the great enterprise, and eloquent pens have told the thrilling story in every variety of picturesque detail. But of the voyage of Cabot, fraught with such vast results, almost nothing is known. The records which have floated down to us were written long after the event, and are of the most meagre and unsatisfactory description. Hence, while from the writings of Columbus and those of his contemporaries, we are able to form a vivid idea of the man himself, of his heroic character and great achievements, so that his name is a household word and his life-history a part of our literature, John Cabot is a mere shadow looming dimly from the darkness of the past. He has been, till recently, almost forgotten; his great discoveries overlooked, and his services to England and humanity ignored. No honours have been paid to his memory, and it is only now, after a lapse of four hundred years, that the public conscience seems to be awakening to the injustice done to the name and memory of a great man, and that the wrongs of centuries seem likely to be righted. "The great soul of the world is just," no doubt; but it is often uphill work to convince the world as to who have been its true benefactors and are entitled to its admiration and reverence. Too often the prophets and benefactors of the world are first stoned, and their sepulchres are built by after-generations. Cabot's hour has come at last; and the accumulated dust of centuries will be cleared away from his memory, and due honours paid to the man who pioneered the way for the English-speaking race who have now overspread the continent of North America.

Not for a moment would we attempt to detract from the glories that encircle the great name of Columbus. His achievement must be regarded as the most important in the annals of the world. He raised the curtain that shrouded the abysses of the Western Ocean, and revealed a New World of boundless wealth and marvellous extent and beauty. He at once doubled the habitable globe, and gave a new direction to men's thoughts and efforts. He established a connection which could never be lost or destroyed between two hemispheres. It was a noble deed which could never be repeated; and for all time must encircle the name of the doer with imperishable renown.

One brave deed leads to others. The grand achievement of Columbus fired the soul of John Cabot with the idea that he, too, could do something great for the honour and advantage of his adopted country. The thought that possessed his mind was that by taking a north-west course across the Atlantic, instead of the south-west route of Columbus, he would reach, by a shorter voyage, the eastern coasts of Asia. He hoped to open up intercourse with China and Japan, or, as they were named by Marco Polo, Cathay and Cipango. Like Columbus, he achieved far more than he dreamed of. He little suspected that between him and the eastern coasts of Asia there lay a vast continent and the waters of the Pacific Ocean. But the glory of his achievement lay in this—that he was the first who saw the mainland of the American continent; and a year before Columbus touched the margin of that continent in the neighbourhood of Veragua, and before Amerigo Vespucci made his first voyage across the Atlantic, Cabot landed on its shores and coasted them for hundreds of miles. His hoped-for communication with China and Japan, in this direction, had to be adjourned for three hundred and fifty years; but by the energy and enterprise of the English-speaking race, whose way he had pioneered, this intercourse has at length been established. Roads of steel, steam-driven vessels, and telegraphic wires have linked Cathay and Cipango to England and the rest of the world across the continent of North America and the waters of the vast Pacific. The old idea has been realized in a new and more fully-developed form. "There is nothing new under the sun." After four hundred years the western path to Cipango and Cathay has been found.

The discovery of Cabot was only second in greatness to that of Columbus. Indeed, in some respects the former had the more difficult task. While the path of Columbus lay in genial climes, amid summer seas and pleasant breezes, Cabot's course led him across the North Atlantic, the stormiest sea in the world, strewn with icebergs and icefields, and often swept by fierce tempests. While the course of Columbus, ever bending to the south-west, brought him into "the Mar de Damas, the Ladies' Sea," where with "the blue above and the blue below," there is almost perpetual summer, and storms are nearly unknown, Cabot had to face the scowling waves of a grim unknown sea, with its fogs and dangerous currents, and grope his way without knowing where land would be found. Columbus had the Azores as a half-way port; Cabot had two thousand miles of unbroken ocean, never furrowed by European keel since the days of the Norsemen, five hundred years before. Equally with Columbus he had to confront the dark unknown, but under greater perils, where, as Pasqualigo informs us, "he wandered about for a long time." It needed a stout heart and a resolute spirit to launch out into these wild waters for the first time, in a little caravel—a mere cockle-shell—in which most men would now hesitate to take even a short coasting voyage. But Cabot and his bold West-Country sailors did not quail, and they have placed their names high on the rolls of fame, by conquering a new world for England.

For in point of fact, the day on which the *Matthew* sailed from the port of Bristol was a historic moment, on which hung the destinies of millions. Cabot, as we have seen, was the real discoverer of North America. In virtue of his discoveries, England established her claim to the sovereignty of a large portion of these northern lands.

That passion for colonization which has since dotted the globe with English colonies was then first kindled. In Newfoundland, and as a consequence of Cabot's discovery, England was afterwards to try "her 'prentice hand" in planting colonies. Here was her eldest-born colony, "the beginning of her strength;" and the "swarming" tendency thus developed has gone on deepening and strengthening ever since. Never was it so productive of important results as in this year, when the various colonies scattered over the world will join in celebrating the sixtieth anniversary of Queen Victoria's accession to the throne, and will send their representatives to London to take part in a gorgeous ceremonial which has no parallel in the historic records of the Empire.

That England is now a world-empire, and not confined to her own small islands and narrow seas, but has spread her millions of sons and daughters over both hemispheres, is largely owing to Cabot's great discovery. It led, first of all, to the occupation of a large portion of the northern continent. The fish-wealth of the surrounding seas first attracted English fishermen. Battling the billows, these hardy fishermen became expert and fearless sailors, built up the British navy, and laid the foundations of that sea-power and maritime supremacy which England has preserved from the days of Elizabeth to those of Victoria. Enormous wealth was drawn from those North American fisheries. For their protection colonies were first planted, and these led on to greater developments. Other nations, such as France, came to share in the spoils, but were finally compelled to retire from the field. To the daring genius of the Cabots we largely owe it that North America is to-day almost entirely occupied by an English-speaking population, with all their vast energies and accumulated wealth. The honour of England was pledged to keep what the daring enterprise of her seamen had discovered. But for this voyage of Cabot and his Gloucester and Devon sailors, Spain might for a long time have monopolized discovery in North as well as South America. English and French enterprise might have taken different directions, and the history of North America might have been shaped in a different fashion. England might not have developed into a great mother of colonies, and failed to become the dominant sea-power of the world, and the ruler of the waves. The coming of the little *Matthew* into these western waters heralded the approaching supremacy of the English race.

All this was the outcome of the Cabot voyages. His is, therefore, a name to be honoured wherever the English tongue is spoken and the flag of England floats. John Cabot is worthy of the noblest celebration we can give him on his fourth centenary. On this point we can quote the highest living authority—that of Sir Clements R. Markham, President of the Royal Geographical Society of England, who says, in a recent letter to the Royal Society of Canada, " It is fitting that the memorable achievement of that intrepid seaman, John Cabot, should be remembered on the four hundredth anniversary of his discovery, and it seems to me specially fitting that a commemoration should take place in the land which he was the first to discover.

"There is great significance in the voyage of Cabot. It was not the first British enterprise of the kind; for during the previous seven years expeditions had been annually despatched from Bristol to discover land to the westward. But it was the first that was led by a man possessed of all the scientific knowledge of his time, and the first that was successful.

"John Cabot must, therefore, be considered to have been the founder of British maritime enterprise. It is unfortunate that nothing has been preserved that can give us a clear idea of the man, of his character and his attainments. John Cabot is little more than a name; but it is a great name. The few certain facts we know concerning him are immortal facts, ever to be had in remembrance. He made the third voyage across the Atlantic, and returned. He discovered the mainland of America. He raised the beacon which showed Englishmen the way to the New World. He was the first to hoist the cross of St. George on the western side of the Atlantic. His fate is unknown. Scarcely anything is known of his companions. But the names of three Englishmen are preserved, who certainly fitted out vessels, and probably went with Cabot in 1498. The names of Lancelot Thirkill, Thomas Bradley, and John Carter, therefore, should also be had in remembrance.

"There are very solid reasons for a Cabot celebration, very complete justifications of the proposals of the Royal Society of Canada. I trust the proposal will receive the support it deserves, and I can assure you that this honour done to the memory of the great navigator has my most cordial sympathy, and I am sure that it will have the sympathy of the Society over which I have the honour to preside."

Another authority may be referred to. Mr. J. F. Nicholls, City Librarian of Bristol, has written an excellent memoir of Sebastian Cabot, whose name, together with those of his two brothers, was associated with that of his father, John Cabot, in the Letters Patent granted by Henry VII. Nicholls holds that Sebastian took part with his father in the great enterprise of discovery, and carried it on after his death; that "he was the most scientific seaman of his own, or perhaps many subsequent ages;" that he was the father of free trade and rendered many great services to England in after-years. "And yet," adds his biographer, "he who gave to England a continent and to Spain an empire (Brazil) lies in some unknown grave. This man, who surveyed and depicted three thousand miles of coast which he had discovered; who gave to Britain not only the continent but the untold riches of the deep in the fisheries of Newfoundland, and the whale-fishery of the Arctic Sea; who by his uprightness and fair dealing raised England's name high among the nations, placed her credit on a solid foundation, and made her citizens respected; who gave her the carrying trade of the world;—this man has not a statue in the city that gave him birth or in the metropolis of the country he so greatly enriched, or a name in the land he discovered. One of the gentlest, bravest, best of men—his actions have been misrepresented, his discoveries denied, his deeds ascribed to others, and calumny has flung its filth on his memory."

This reproach will now be wiped away. "The whirligig of Time brings in his revenges." On the four hundredth anniversary of his discovery the names of John and Sebastian Cabot will be recalled with highest honours; permanent monuments will be erected to their memories, and eloquent lips will sound their praises.

The curtain now rises on a little caravel—a mere speck on the world of waters—struggling westward. Pacing its deck, vigilant, hopeful, resolute, is the heroic man who is about to throw open the gates of the North Atlantic. Is there not a moral grandeur around him as with eyes kindling with the fires of faith and hope, blessing every breeze that wafts him from the abodes of civilized men, his resolution inexorable as doom, he boldly sails westward, far beyond the bounds where the most daring have ventured before? The rude winds pursue their wild revels, indifferent to his fortunes; the black billows leap around his little barque, threatening to swallow it up; but the heroic heart refuses to turn back. The invisible seems to whisper, "Onward." His triumph gleams from afar. A hand is stretched out to him from the darkness and he grasps it. His prophetic eye sees the fair lands to which he is opening the pathway.

Still it was a hard battle, and doubtless hope often wavered. For fifty-two days the tiny craft had been struggling with the waves, and still there was not the faintest indication that land was near. But as the sun rose on the morning of the fifty-third day—the 24th of June—the welcome cry of "Land Ho!" rang out from the mast-head of the *Matthew*, and West-Country sailors greeted the sight of the new land with hearty English cheers. It was a memorable day, only second in importance to that on which Columbus and his companions gazed on the shores of San Salvador.

CHAPTER II.

A Missing Chapter in History—Cabot's Reward—Meagre Records of his Voyage—The Landfall—Difficulty of determining it—Competing theories—Cabot's Second Voyage, 1498—Historical injustice to Sebastian Cabot—Estimate of his Character and Work —Cabot the Discoverer of Newfoundland—Object of the Fourth Centenary Celebration.

HAD there been on board the *Matthew* a capable chronicler to record faithfully the events of that momentous voyage, one of the most stirring and delightful stories in the annals of early maritime adventures might have been given to the world. We cannot believe that those fifty-three days spent by John Cabot and his companions tossing amid the rough billows of the North Atlantic, and groping for land in its unknown wildernesses, were dull, monotonous, and uneventful. The man who was now opening vast fields for human enterprise and energy, and providing new homes for the crowded populations of Europe, and giving us the waves for our ships, though of heroic mould, was "a man of like passions with ourselves." He must have had, on that perilous voyage, moments of doubt and gloom, when his enthusiasm flagged, and the star of hope was eclipsed for a time. Storms may have threatened the destruction of his frail barque, and many an anxious hour may have been spent peering into those frowning Western billows. As he got farther and farther into the abysses and no signs of land appeared, it may have been that the hearts of his sailors, though naturally stout and brave, began to fail, and the dread crept over them that this mad enthusiast was leading them to destruction, and that they would see their English homes no more. And so it may have happened that, like Columbus, he had to cheer and strengthen the timid and weak, and wrestle with cowardice and mutiny that would have forced him to turn back. If any such tendencies showed themselves among his crew, a glance from that calm clear eye would be sufficient to quell all mutinous spirits; and that commanding voice, thundering out his orders, who would dare to disobey? He has come out to find land in the West, and, by the blessing of Heaven, he will press on and finish his task. He has need of all his patient fortitude and stern resolve, for he is alone "the beating heart of this great enterprise."

In imagination we see this sea-king, of grave and lofty bearing, his face lighted up with enthusiasm as, day after day, and week after week, he paces the deck. He is greater than all this tumultuous waste of waters around him, for, like Columbus, he has the soul of a hero and a strong trust in God. The long arms of his faith have reached across and already touched the promised land. Then, as the sun goes down, and night closes in, we can see him in his little cabin, with the flickering light of a poor lamp, poring over Toscannelli's map of the world—the highest geographical authority of those days; and then opening the marvellous pages of Marco Polo, and pondering his glowing descriptions of Cipango and Cathay—the lands to which he firmly believed he was now approaching. In the quaint pages of the old traveller he sees gleaming the foreshadowings of his own high hopes, and his faith grasps "the land that is very far off."

But of all that occurred on board the *Matthew*—of the hopes and fears, the struggles and disappointments of those on board—we know absolutely nothing. If any records were made, or any diary kept on board, they are buried deep in the waves of time, and it is very unlikely any of them will now be recovered. This missing chapter in world-history is gone irrecoverably, and we are so much the poorer. In all Hakluyt's invaluable records of the voyages of these old days, which he has preserved, there is none we should not be willing to exchange for the story of John Cabot's voyage.

How we should like to know with what sort of welcome these English sailors greeted the first sight of land; how they gathered round their brave commander with cheers and congratulations; and with what ceremonial forms Cabot landed and planted in the soil the flag of England, that of St. Mark, being a citizen of Venice, and also a large cross; thus unconsciously taking possession of a continent for his sovereign. But of this momentous event we have but the briefest record by the hand of an Italian merchant in London, who met Cabot on his return. "The English," said Carlyle, "are a dumb people. They can do great acts but not describe them. Like the old Romans and some few others, their epic poem is written on the earth's service: England—her mark."

Cabot gave to the spot where he landed the name of *Prima Vista*. There is no reason for supposing that he, any more than Columbus, knew of the greatness of his discovery, or even suspected that he had touched the margin of a new continent. He reported, on his return, that he had reached the territory of the Grand Khan; so that, like Columbus, he thought the western coasts of the Atlantic, where he landed, were the eastern coasts of Asia.

After spending some twelve or fourteen days in exploring further along the coast, Cabot turned his prow homeward, his provisions probably running low; and on the 6th of August he arrived at Bristol, having been absent ninety-six days.

The great news spread of the discovery of land to the west, but it does not appear to have awakened any great enthusiasm in Bristol. No cheering multitudes, or waving flags, or salvos of artillery greeted Cabot on landing after his memorable voyage. So far as known, his return received no public notice, and called forth no popular rejoicings. His discovery was neither understood nor appreciated. Probably his voyage was considered a failure, as it brought no immediate gain— no news of gold or prospects of profitable trade. Two Bristol chroniclers, however, took the trouble of making a note of the event. One old manuscript, still in existence, records that, " This year (1497), on St. John the Baptist's day, the land of America * was found by the

---

* "America" is, of course, a later interpolation if the extract is really genuine.

merchants of Bristowe, in a ship of Bristowe called the *Matthew*, the which ship departed from the port of Bristowe on the 2nd day of May, and came home again the 6th of August following." Another Bristol manuscript has the following record, in briefer terms: "In the year 1497, the 24th of June, on St. John's day, was Newfoundland found by Bristol men in a ship called the *Matthew*." Both of these ancient documents agree as to the date of the discovery of land and the name of the ship, and both fail to mention the discoverer whose genius and courage pointed the way which so many thousands have since followed. Such too often is fame among contemporaries. The world's great men —the benefactors of their race—are too frequently, when living, treated with neglect or bitter contempt; but after-generations recognize their merits and do justice to their memories. Bristol will this year make amends for its neglect of the living Cabot. On the fourth centenary of his discovery a statue of its greatest citizen will be unveiled in Bristol, and a noble orator will pronounce his eulogium, and twine fresh wreaths of *immortelles* around his name.

It would appear that Cabot made but a brief stay in Bristol, and went on to London, no doubt to report himself to King Henry. What was his reception here? Did his grateful sovereign summon him to his royal palace and, in the midst of his assembled courtiers, listen to the tale of his marvellous achievement, give him thanks for the immense service done to the realm, and heap rewards and honours on his head? No such thing. Henry sent him ten pounds; and lest posterity should forget his generosity, he hastened to make an entry of this benefaction in his Privy Purse accounts, which are still to be seen in the British Museum, in the following curt terms: "August 10th, 1497.—To Hym that found the New Isle, £10." He little thought that by this entry he was posting his own mean penuriousness for the scorn of posterity. His stinginess is made more flagrant by the fact that in the patent he granted to the Cabots he stipulated that the enterprise should be carried out "upon their own proper costes and charges," but that "the aforesaid John and his sonnes and heirs be bounden of all the fruits, gaines, and commodities growing of such navigation, to pay unto us, in wares or money, the fifth part of the capital gain so gotten." Never did a monarch obtain a continent on such easy terms.

What a different reception was accorded to Columbus, five years before, when he entered the port of Palos, bringing the news of his great discovery, amid the ringing plaudits of a vast multitude. Ferdinand and Isabella awaited him in Barcelona, and his march thither was a triumphal procession, like that of a Roman conqueror. Joy-bells rang as he passed through the towns, the people crowding the house-tops to obtain a sight of the great discoverer. Seated on their thrones, under a rich canopy of brocade of gold, Ferdinand and Isabella were ready to receive the hero of the hour. As he entered the magnificent saloon they rose to receive him, bade him be seated in their presence, and having listened to his wondrous story, the august assembly fell on their knees and gave thanks to God with many tears, and then rose and chanted the "Te Deum." The poor Genoese sailor was in that hour the most famous and honoured man in all the world.

Away in the cold and stormy north, many hundreds of miles from the sunny lands found by Columbus, John Cabot, five years later, opened a pathway for a far nobler civilization than that of the south. An English-speaking host followed in his track in due time, and occupied the continent. When he went home with the news, the "dumb English" received him in silence, as if he had done nothing great; and their king gave him ten pounds as a token of his satisfaction. Perhaps it is a mark of the true greatness of the English race—of their solid strength—that they shrink from giving way to their emotions or huzzaing over a great man or a great deed. Though they recognize both, and appreciate true worth, and admire profoundly a noble deed, they often prefer to do so in silence. As Kipling puts it—

> "Deeper than speech our love,
>   Stronger than life our tether,
> We do not fall on the neck,
>   Nor kiss when we come together.
>
> "Go to your work and be strong,
>   Halting not in your ways,
> Baulking the end half-won,
>   For an instant dole of praise.
>
> "Stand to your work and be wise,
>   Certain of sword and pen,
> Who are neither children nor gods,
>   But men in a world of men."

Still the silent English are not ungrateful. Though

they may be slow and dull in discovering merit, in due time the prophet's sepulchre is built and the hero's monument erected, and *immortelles* are laid on the tomb of the illustrious dead. They did not know at first what a great and noble work Cabot had accomplished; and he was received coldly, and in a few years almost forgotten. There was no monument to keep his memory alive. But the fourth centenary arrives, and the name of Cabot is on every tongue.

The shouts in Spain welcoming Columbus soon died away. Malice and envy did their work; and only seven years after his triumphal entry into Barcelona, the great man again reached Palos from the scene of his discoveries, a prisoner and in chains—the result of false and calumnious charges made by the wretched Bobadilla. It is true the fetters were struck off and the ungrateful treatment was repudiated by the monarch; yet in the hero's old age the same Ferdinand treated him with coldness and neglect; refused to restore his offices, dignities, and property of which he had been unjustly deprived, and left him to die in poverty and neglect.

The personal treatment accorded to John Cabot was by no means so bad as this. There is an old letter which was brought to light in Milan, written by Lorenzo Pasqualigo, a Venetian gentleman then resident in London. It bears the date of August 23, 1497, and is addressed to his brother in Venice. In it the writer says, "This Venetian of ours went in a ship from Bristol in quest of new islands, is returned, and says that seven hundred leagues hence he discovered *terra firma*, which is the territory of the Great Khan. The king is much pleased with this intelligence. He has also given him money wherewith to amuse himself, and he is now in Bristol with his wife, who is a Venetian woman, and with his sons. His name is Zuan Cabot, and they call him the Great Admiral. Vast honour is paid to him, and he dresses in silk; and these English run after him like mad people, so that he can enlist as many of them as he pleases."

It would appear from this record that the achievement of John Cabot touched the heart of the people, whatever Henry and his courtiers may have thought of it. But the shoutings of a street crowd soon died away, and the king's present of ten pounds (equal in purchasing power to about one hundred pounds of our currency) was soon exhausted in the pleasures of a brief holiday; and in a few years Cabot's name was almost forgotten.

It would, no doubt, be very gratifying if we knew with certainty the exact spot on which Cabot landed and planted the banner of St. George. To erect his statue, or some suitable monument, on that spot, on the fourth centenary of his discovery, would be an act of historic justice, redressing, as far as we are able, the wrongs of the past. But even this is impossible. Nothing approaching to absolute certainty regarding his landfall is now attainable. Historians and antiquarians differ widely on this point. It is certain that Cabot made a record of his landing-place. In the State Archives of Milan a letter has been found, some thirty years ago, in which Raimondo di Soncino, writing under date, 18th of December, 1497, to the Duke of Milan, says, among other things, "This Messer Zoanne Caboto has the description of the world in a chart, and also in a solid globe which he has made, and he shows where he landed." The Spanish envoys, Puebla and Ayala, writing between August 24th, 1497, and July 25th, 1498, mention having seen such a chart and globe, but unfortunately they are lost. It can hardly be doubted that Sebastian Cabot afterwards would write an account of his father's voyage and delineate his course on a chart. Writing in 1582, some twenty-five years after his death, Hakluyt tells us that Sebastian Cabot's papers were then "in the custody of William Worthington, and were shortly to be printed." In some mysterious way they disappeared, and not a fragment of them is known to be in existence, and not a solitary line written by John or Sebastian Cabot has escaped the wrecks of time. It is not wonderful, therefore, that, with such meagre and fragmentary records of contemporaries as are left us, there should be such a diversity of opinion in regard to Cabot's landfall. Even in the case of Columbus's landfall, though all the records have been carefully preserved, there is still a difference of opinion, though it seems now to be generally allowed that Watling Island, and not San Salvador, as was once believed, was the spot on which he landed. Captain Fox, however, of the United States navy, still argues for Samana; Navarelte for Grand Turk's Island; and Irving and Humboldt for Cat Island.

Among historians and geographers there are at present

three leading theories as to Cabot's landfall. Some place it at Cape Bonavista, on the eastern coast of Newfoundland. Others hold that it was on the coast of Labrador, but differ widely as to the latitude of the place; while an increasing number of writers argue in favour of the most eastern point of Cape Breton Island. The most recent and the most careful researches point in the direction of the last-named locality as the true landfall, and by some of the ablest authorities probabilities are now pronounced to be strongly in its favour. Mathematical demonstration on such a point is, of course, out of the question; moral certainty alone is attainable. But the evidence now accumulated, chiefly from a study of the oldest and most reliable maps, reaches a high degree of probability; while an impartial examination of the proofs presented by the supporters of the other two theories shows that they are entirely insufficient.

In regard to Bonavista, in Newfoundland, its claim rests on a vague tradition or assumption, for which no tangible proof can be adduced. Probably the name, which is Portuguese, suggested to after-generations that "happy sight" must also have signified "first sight," and that, therefore, "Bonavista" must have been the first land seen by Cabot. The mistake crept into general literature, and has been repeated by many writers who did not give the matter any consideration. But it must be remembered that Cabot was himself an Italian, sailing on a voyage of discovery under the patent of an English monarch, and with an English crew, and was, therefore, very unlikely to give a Portuguese name to his landfall.

In favour of the Labrador theory many high authorities might be cited, and much strong evidence adduced. But, without going into the controversy at any length, there seems to be one insuperable objection to Labrador having been the landfall of Cabot's first voyage. He made land on the 24th of June. At that date the coast of Labrador is beset by ice and icebergs at the alleged latitudes—56° to 58°—and is rarely, if ever, accessible so early in summer, especially by vessels approaching from the eastward. Even now, no captain of a sailing vessel would think of venturing so far North at such a date. In any case, Cabot, had he made his way to this part of the coast on the 24th of June, must have seen immense quantities of ice. Now we have several accounts of the first voyage, the most reliable being that of Pasqualigo. He mentions that Cabot saw "felled trees, snares for catching game," and speaks of " the tides being slack," but makes no mention of ice or any difficulties connected with it. Had he met with icebergs or icefields, such a remarkable phenomenon could not have been forgotten. Even if we take the lowest latitude named by the supporters of this theory—53° or 54°—the ice difficulty still presents itself. Further, John Cabot told Soncino "that the land he found was excellent, and the climate temperate, suggesting that Brazil wood and silk grow there;" and that on the 24th of June! Such considerations seem to render Labrador entirely improbable as Cabot's landfall.

The positive evidence in favour of the Cape Breton theory is cumulative, and derived from several reliable sources, and, in the aggregate, presents such a formidable array that it will be found difficult, if not impossible, to set it aside. Dr. S. E. Dawson, of Ottawa, in an exhaustive monograph, read before the Royal Society of Canada in 1894, and in a sequel presented in 1896, has massed this evidence so skilfully and impartially that, to the writer, he seems to have settled the long-debated question. No source of information has been left unexamined, and Dr. Dawson's local knowledge of the region, and of the adjacent islands and coasts, is turned to admirable account; while his refutation of competing theories is complete. No one who wishes to study the vexed question should overlook these important papers, which appear in the "Transactions of the Royal Society of Canada."

It is outside the scope of this small volume to enter minutely into such a controversy. It will be sufficient to state that Dr. Dawson rests his argument mainly on the famous map made in 1500 by the Biscayan pilot, Juan de La Cosa, who sailed with Columbus on his first and second voyages. The importance of this map in determining Cabot's landfall can hardly be overrated. Fiske, in his "Discovery of America," says, "So far as is known, this is the earliest map in existence made since 1492, and its importance is very great. La Casa calls La Cosa the best pilot of his day. His reputation as a cartographer is also high, and his maps are much admired. This map is evidently drawn with honesty and care." By a careful study of this map, combined with many other sources of information, Dr. Dawson has reached the conclusion that the most eastern point of Cape Breton Island, indicated on this map as "Cavo Descubierto"—"the discovered cape"—is the *prima tierra vista*. He also shows that, "as this map of La Cosa's was, beyond all reasonable doubt, based on John Cabot's own map, which Pedro de Ayala, the Spanish Ambassador, had from him, and promised in July, 1498, to send to King Ferdinand, we have here John Cabot indicating his own landfall in a Spanish translation." This is also the opinion of Sir Clements Markham.

Dr. Dawson uses also the celebrated "Sebastian Cabot Map" of 1544, about which so much controversy has raged, in corroboration of his views. The latter map, as is well known, places the landfall at Cape North, the northern point of Cape Breton Island. Although many very high authorities hold the Cabot Map of 1544 to be authentic, yet, for reasons given, Dr. Dawson prefers the authority of the La Cosa Map, while regarding the other as of much interest and importance.

A second patent was granted solely to John Cabot by Henry VII., dated February 3rd, 1498, authorizing him to sail with six ships "to the land and isles of late found by the said John in our name and by our commandment." This patent was evidently a supplementary commission. Strange to say, from this date John Cabot's name disappears from contemporary records. Whether his death took place before the expedition was ready, or soon after its return, we know not. No satisfactory record of this second voyage by Cabot has been preserved. A letter from Pedro de Ayala, the Spanish envoy then in England, and an entry in Stow's Chronicle, make it certain that the expedition sailed early in the summer of 1498, and had not returned in the following September. In fact, there is no authentic account of its return; but from the pages of Peter Martyr, Ramusio, Gomara, and Galvano we learn that on this voyage Cabot sailed far along the Labrador coast till stopped by masses of ice; that he then turned south and followed the coast to 38° N., thus discovering from twelve hundred to eighteen hundred miles of the coast of North America; and that, in virtue of this, England in due time claimed sovereignty over these northern lands by right of a first discovery.

It is curious to note how historians have dealt with the memory of the elder and younger Cabot. For a long period the father's name was ignored and almost effaced in connection with the great discovery, while the son's name was unduly and unjustly exalted, as though he had been the prime mover and the ruling spirit in carrying through the great enterprise. It was even declared to be doubtful whether John Cabot had sailed on the first voyage at all, or that he took any part in the second, so that the whole glory belonged of right to Sebastian. Indiscriminating praise was lavished on the latter, while the name of the elder was entirely suppressed. The injudicious zeal of ardent admirers in uncritical times led writers like Biddle, Nicholl, and others to exaggerate the merits of Sebastian and to paint him as a paragon of excellence. In more recent times fresh documents have been brought to light, chiefly from Spanish archives, which have completely turned the scale, and re-established the reputation of John Cabot on a solid foundation—proving him to have been the real discoverer and the moving spirit in the whole enterprise—a man, too, of a noble spirit and courageous heart. Now the rebound seems to have gone too far, and some are disposed to deny all merit to the son, and even refuse to believe that he had any part in the discovery. His character has been assailed, and he has been painted as an unmitigated liar, an impostor, and one who endeavoured to deprive his father of his well-earned fame. Even nautical skill has been denied him. The eminent historian and antiquarian, Harrisse, has gone to great and unwarrantable extremes in his violent onslaught on the memory of Sebastian Cabot. As usual, the truth lies between the two extremes. The reputation of Sebastian Cabot has suffered not only from eulogiums of over-zealous friends, but also from the fact that no record from his own hand has escaped the gnawing tooth of time. We are dependent for information regarding the second voyage, and the utterances and after-career of Sebastian, on the works of men who wrote long afterwards, and wrote from memory, such as Ramusio and Gomara, and whose recollections may have been dim and incorrect. Memory, in such cases, is apt to prove treacherous after a lapse of years; or the writers may have partially misunderstood the voyager, and unintentionally misrepresented his statements. They did not know the whole case. Some of them knew only about the voyage of 1498, nothing of the earlier one; others confounded the two voyages. It is unfair to condemn Sebastian and to brand him as an unscrupulous falsifier on certain conversations which these writers say they held with him. We have not the whole case before us; and many of his reported statements may have admitted of explanations, had we the means of sifting them. If we merely pick out flaws, imperfections, and failings in a man's character, we shall form a very false estimate of the man; for the best of men have plenty of weaknesses and imperfections, and often yield to selfish considerations or gusts of passion. The heroic Columbus was far enough from perfection; and, as some ungracious writers have tried to show, was guilty of some very questionable deeds. But allowance is made for the influences of his age and training; and, notwithstanding these, we admire and reverence the hero for his solid worth and true nobility of soul.

We must take into account that Sebastian Cabot lived in the close of the fifteenth and beginning of the sixteenth century; at a time when a high sense of honour and a moral obligation to tell the truth were by no means general even among educated and eminent men; and when deception and lying did not meet with that keen and instant condemnation which they merit. Scheming, intriguing, and finessing were widely prevalent; and even at the close of our refined nineteenth century it is to be feared that they are not quite unknown. A fine sense of veracity and reverence for truth and fact are among the last blossomings of an age of Christian culture. Cabot could not escape being tainted more or less by the vices of his age, and influenced in his conduct by the prevalent ideas of his time. But to seize on some apparent or real transgressions of the laws of veracity, and hunt him down and condemn him for these, is to misjudge and deal unfairly with the man. He had his failings, no doubt; but that he was the pertinacious liar and incompetent pretender that Harrisse has tried to paint him is entirely incredible. He intrigued at times in a discreditable manner for selfish ends; he was guilty of want of candour and concealment of facts more than once, we may admit; but it must be remembered we have no opportunity of cross-examining the witnesses against him. Still he was a brave and able man who did a great work for the world, and, on the whole, in a noble spirit. If we withhold our respect from him and condemn him for certain flaws of character, what great man can we reverence?

For consider the broad facts of the case. His name was associated with that of his father in Henry's patent. That he accompanied his father on his first voyage is in the highest degree probable, though the few meagre records do not expressly say so. From the fact that his father's name totally disappears from contemporary records, and that he is not mentioned as ever returning from the second voyage, we may fairly infer that his death took place at that time, and that Sebastian commanded the second expedition. It is well known that Sebastian's ruling passion was to find a passage to Cathay by the north-west. Hence his father's original programme was altered, and in his second voyage he boldly steered to the north-west, and fought the ice-floes and icebergs along the rugged coast of Labrador as far north as Hudson's Strait. Thus to Sebastian Cabot must be accorded the honour of pioneering the way in Arctic exploration, and of kindling in the bosoms of Englishmen that passion for Arctic discovery in which they have surpassed all others, and put on record deeds of heroic bravery which have won imperishable renown. Sebastian Cabot led the way, and a long line of Arctic heroes followed, the latest being the gallant Nansen. When compelled to turn back by the ice and intense cold, he sailed south as far as 38° N., thus discovering the whole coast of North America, from Hudson's Strait to Florida—an event, as we have seen, of the first magnitude in connection with the settlement of the continent.

Some time after his return to England he was invited by Ferdinand of Spain to enter his service. He had no reason to consider himself under any obligations to England. His discoveries had not yet been understood or appreciated by the English, and no objections were raised to his transference of his services in 1512 to Spain. Ferdinand gave him an honourable position and a salary of 50,000 maravedis per annum. He wanted to turn to account Sebastian's knowledge of the Baccalaos, or New Fish Lands, which was considered of little or no value in England. Who could blame him, under such circumstances, for removing to Spain and accepting an office of honour and emolument—that of Grand Pilot of Spain and Head of the Department of Cartography at Seville? This office he held with credit to himself till 1546, both under Ferdinand and Charles—two of the ablest monarchs of those days, and excellent judges of character. Had Sebastian been the incompetent sham represented by Harrisse, would such shrewd judges of men and affairs not have speedily seen through him and given him his dismissal, instead of honouring him as they did for thirty-four years ?

During those years Sebastian Cabot made several more voyages of discovery, actively promoted maritime enterprises and trading adventures, and by invitation took part in the famous conference at Badajos. In his old age he returned to England, and Edward VI. bestowed on him a pension of £166 as a mark of respect. His mental activity and interest in maritime affairs continued to the last, and he died in London, probably about 1557, when close on eighty years of age.

In view of all these facts, there seems to be no reason why on the fourth Cabot centenary the name of Sebastian Cabot should not be joined with that of his illustrious father, though of the two we may be bound to accord the higher honour to the memory of John Cabot, who was undoubtedly the originator and leader in the first voyage. His son, however, is entitled to high praise for brave and daring deeds, and to an honoured place in the roll of England's illustrious sailors. After the lapse of four hundred years it seems unjust and ungracious to " draw his frailties from their dread abode," and ignore his vast services to the English race, and overlook the part he took in the expansion of England.

Although the theory that Newfoundland was Cabot's landfall must be abandoned as untenable, yet no one has ever doubted or denied that he discovered the island on his first voyage, and was the first to report the immense fish-wealth of its surrounding seas. Newfoundland is bound to honour the memory of Cabot as its discoverer, and will take a worthy part in celebrating the fourth Cabot centenary. How much of the island he saw cannot be determined; but the fact of discovery is indisputable, and the name, "New-Found-land," which included at first the adjacent coasts and islands, was finally appropriated to the island which still bears the name.

Still it must be admitted that no critical authority of eminence can be cited in support of the theory that Newfoundland was Cabot's landfall. Harrisse, who has made a most extensive and minute examination of the old documents connected with the discovery of America, does not even mention or discuss it. In his earlier works he held that the landfall was on the eastern coast of Cape Breton; but in his latest he fixes on Cape Chidley, the most northern point of Labrador—an impossible landfall, as we have seen, on the 24th of June. For Newfoundland, however, he does not seem to consider there was any evidence whatever.

On the other hand, many of the most eminent geographers and historians may be quoted as supporters of the Cape Breton view. Sir Clements Markham, President of the Royal Geographical Society, Dr. Beurinot, Dr. Charles Deane, the Abbé J. D. Beaudoin,

ICEBERG.

Francesco Tarducci, an eminent Italian historian, Brevoort, an American author, and Dr. S. E. Dawson, all support the Cape Breton landfall. But the important point is that Cabot, by his discovery, united Newfoundland to England, that the tie has never been severed since, and that the loyalty and devotion of England's oldest colony to the throne and the Empire have never wavered, and on this sixtieth anniversary of the glorious reign of Queen Victoria are as warm and true as ever.

Except as a matter of historical or antiquarian interest, the mere spot where Cabot first saw land is not of any great importance. The map of La Cosa shows that on his return voyage Cabot coasted along the southern shore of Newfoundland for three hundred miles and named it, thus closely identifying himself and his famous voyage with the island. The landfall, about which there will, perhaps, always be a difference of opinion, is comparatively a minor point; the centenary celebration commemorates the discovery of North America—one of the great landmarks of history.

CHAPTER III.

Reverence for our noble dead—Union of England's Ocean-Empire—Her need of her Colonies—Homes for an increasing Population—Mistakes of the Past in dealing with the Colonies—Beginnings in Newfoundland—The Fishing Era—Bretons and Basques first—The English follow—Expansion of English Fishing at Newfoundland—Genesis of Settlement—Value of Fisheries—Results—Sir Humphrey Gilbert takes possession of the Island—His heroic Death—Loss to Newfoundland—Queen Elizabeth and Queen Victoria—The Colonies in Victoria's Reign—Free Institutions.

MAX MÜLLER, in his "Chips from a German Workshop," tells us that, "In this cold and critical age of ours, the power of worshipping, the art of admiring, the passion of loving what is great and good, are fast dying out." When we recall the homage paid to the memory of Columbus four years ago, and the magnificence with which his fourth centenary was celebrated, the tribute paid by literature, art, and eloquence to the great discoverer, we might well hesitate to accept the dictum of Max Müller. And when we remember the outburst of admiration and worship which the tercentenary celebration of Shakespeare's birth, some thirty-three years ago, called forth, and the fervid display of reverence for England's greatest poet after he had been three hundred years in his grave; and when we think of the more recent celebration of the centenary of Scotland's national poet all over the civilized world, and the magnificent reception accorded the other day, in London, to the heroic Nansen, we may well doubt the truth of the assertion that mankind are losing the power of admiring and loving their great men. The truly great men who have toiled, and dared, and suffered for humanity, who have raised our souls to higher levels, must and will live on in the love of each successive generation. Such admiration is wholesome and elevating. To think truly, and justly, and reverently of our noble dead will lead many a young heart to emulate their deeds and tread in their footsteps. It is well, therefore, that the present generation should recall the vast services rendered to our English-speaking race by the discoverers of North America, and do homage to their memory, after they slept for four hundred years in their unknown graves. It is an act of tardy justice to them; it is an exercise that will benefit our own souls.

The Cabots led the way in the planting of English Colonies; and it is only now that the value of that work begins to be understood and appreciated, and that Englishmen are awaking to the importance of the colonial portion of the Empire. Happily the day is gone by for treating the Colonies with coldness and neglect. The policy which regarded them as encumbrances, to be cut loose and got rid of so soon as they were able to shift for themselves, has, in the present day, few advocates. A grander idea has gradually taken possession of the minds of the present generation of Englishmen—that of an ocean-empire, in which, throughout Great Britain's vast inheritance, on which the sun never sets, her children may, year after year, spread themselves out, and find healthful, happy, and prosperous homes, still enjoying protection under the old flag, and still regarding the mother-land with loyalty and affection. The policy which English statesmen have now to shape is one that will bind the Colonies in closer bonds of sympathy and good-will to England, and render them integral parts of the Empire, sources of an ever-advancing strength and mutual help and prosperity. The Imperial Federation that will include the Colonies, no doubt, presents many a difficult problem, and may not be immediately attainable; but the first throbbings of the movement are now felt, and gradually the consummation will be reached. The sixtieth anniversary of Her Majesty's reign will give a powerful impulse to a union of her ocean-empire, the effect of which will be felt by coming generations.

England needs the Colonies as truly as they need the helping and protecting hand of England. During the last quarter of a century the Imperial Mother has added seven millions to her population; and, including the increase in her Colonies, the total growth of population in that period has been eleven millions. Homes are wanted for the increasing population of the mother-country, where her millions and tens of millions may find fields of enterprise and labour, and grow up stout of limb, with plenty of iron in their blood and the glow of health in their cheeks, hardened into manly endurance amid the frosts and snows of Canada and Newfoundland, and fitted for the world's hard work under the open skies of Australia and in the vast plains of Southern Africa. The idle hands and the unoccupied lands need to be brought together. England wants ever-advancing communities who will be consumers of her goods and varied manufactures, and among whom she need fear no rival. When the desire for union exists on both sides, who will forbid the banns? When mutual needs and interests draw them together, no adverse force will be able to keep them asunder. Should the day ever come when England will need help against her foes, to whom should she look but to her stalwart sons scattered over her vast outlying domains?

"Look, I have made you a place, and opened wide the doors,
That ye may talk together, your Barons and Councillors—
Wards of the Outer March, Lords of the Lower Seas—
Ay, talk to your grey mother that bore you on her knees!
That ye may talk together, brother to brother's face—
Thus for the good of your peoples—thus for the Pride of the Race.
Also, we will make promise. So long as the Blood endures,
I shall know that your good is mine: ye shall feel that my strength
   is yours;
In the day of Armageddon, at the last great fight of all,
That Our House stand together and the pillars do not fall."*

Other nations are increasing in population, and treading close on the heels of England in their advancing numbers and strength. Germany has added eleven millions to her population during the last twenty-five years. France is behind in the race; but

* Kipling's "Seven Seas."

Russia, Austria, Italy are expanding, and England must grow in order to retain her place in the great march of the nations. But how can such growth be secured and, at the same time, the health and vigour of the race maintained? Not in the British Isles, already filled to overflowing, where land cannot be had in sufficient quantity, and where, in the huge manufacturing cities, millions are living under such unhealthy conditions that degeneracy of race is sufficiently startling already. A strong, capable race, fitted for the world's rough work—a world in which, as Lord Dufferin has lately reminded us, "force, not right, is still the dominant factor in human affairs, and no nation's independence or possessions are safe for a moment unless she can guard them with her own right hand"—this is what England needs if she is to take hostages of the future, and not sink into a second place when she has so long led the van. Her population must increase; but it should be under healthier conditions than those presented in the smoke-canopied cities, the choking factories, the dusty workshops, and the sunless mines. Such free and healthy homes the Colonies present. They could sustain in their ample bosom five times the number of human beings that now crowd the British Isles. Vast areas of fertile soil await cultivators. There are precious minerals to be dragged to the sunlight, and huge forests still untouched by the woodman's axe. Here are ample spaces for the hunger-bitten, unwillingly idle of the old land, to build up happy homes.

But that these emigrants may grow up Englishmen

proud of the name, the fame, and traditions of their race, and ready to stand by the ancient mother in her hour of peril, they must become parts of a united Empire, in which they may feel themselves living members, and not mere appendages, having but a loose and nominal attachment. There is the strongest evidence to show that this is really the desire of a vast majority of colonists. It is for English statesmen to devise the means whereby such union can be secured, and to facilitate the transfer of the people, who will make the Colonial wastes blossom like the rose. It should not be an impossible or even a difficult problem to bring together the fragments of the same nation that are now only separated by distance. Steam and electricity have abolished distance; and the Colonies themselves are already covered with a network of railways. English statesmen have already solved far harder problems than the Federation of the Colonies.

The work of planting English Colonies at first was slow and laborious, and went on through many failures and mistakes during hundreds of years. Strange to say, some of them took root, and grew up not only without aid from successive British Governments, but in spite of them. Such was the case, as we shall see, with Newfoundland. Foolish or selfish laws and restrictions often retarded the growth of a Colony. Englishmen were slow in understanding what was the right use of these settlements in lands beyond the seas. Immediate gain to the mother-country, and the creation of huge monopolies in favour of court favourites or powerful corporations, was too often the main consideration in dealing with the Colonies. And so blunder after blunder went on, till a crisis arrived, and thirteen of Britain's Colonies, goaded into rebellion by tyranny and stupidity on the part of incompetent rulers, threw off their allegiance, and, after torrents of blood had been shed, won their independence. The disgraceful statesmanship that lost to England her American Colonies has proved an instructive object-lesson, and has never been repeated since. More enlightened views as to the relations which ought to subsist between the mother-country and the Colonies gradually established themselves in men's minds; and no collision of any moment has occurred since the War of Independence. At the present moment, under a wiser Administration, England's Colonies are as loyal as any other portions of the Empire, and as firmly bound to her by the ties of affection and sympathy.

Newfoundland and the continent of North America having been discovered by the Cabots, and the flag of England first planted on its soil, the question was raised, What were the English people going to do with their new possessions? If Cabot had told them, on his return, that it was a land where gold and silver could be obtained in abundance, where pearls could be had for the gathering, there would have been an immediate rush to the New-Found-Lands, just as is the case to-day when an auriferous region is reported. But he had no such news to impart. Instead of that, he told them of something infinitely better than the gold mines of Peru and Mexico. He told them that in the waters around these lands there was an abundance of the finest cod and a vast variety of other fishes, such as the eyes of man had never seen before; and that here was a perennial harvest of the sea which only required to be gathered in, and that could never be exhausted. This news was speedily circulated everywhere, and at once arrested attention.

It was a fishing age, in which the consumption of fresh and salted fish was enormous. All Europe—England included—was then Catholic; and during the fasts of the Church, the pickled herring of Holland formed a large item in the diet of the people. Fishing was a lucrative occupation. The foundations of Amsterdam were said to be laid in herring-bones. The Dutch became immensely wealthy by the monopoly of the herring fisheries which they held for a long period. It was no wonder, then, that Cabot's discovery of these great fisheries on the banks and around the shores of Newfoundland created such a sensation, and gave such an impulse to fishing. Persons of the highest distinction took part in the fishing adventures of those days, and freely invested their money in these remunerative industries. Thus the enterprise of the hardy fishermen to procure an article of food for the fast-days of the Church led, as we shall see, to distant enterprises and the settlement of newly-discovered lands, and brought about important political results. Even after England had become Protestant, laws were passed to promote the consumption of fish among the people, in order to encourage the fishing industries, especially those in American waters, and also with an eye to the increase of the navy and mercantile marine. It was the days of sumptuary laws, when people submitted to legal dictation as to what they were to eat, drink, and avoid. In 1563, in the reign of Elizabeth, a law was passed which provided "that as well as for the maintenance of shipping, the increase of fishermen and mariners, and the repairing of port-towns, as for the sparing of the fresh victual of the realm, it shall not be lawful for any one to eat flesh on Wednesdays and Saturdays, unless under the forfeiture of three pounds for each offence, except in case of sickness, and those of special licences to be obtained." Other laws followed until there were one hundred and fifty-three days in the year on which only fish could be eaten. The punishment for the violation of these laws was, for the first offence, a fine of ten shillings and ten days' imprisonment; for the second, double these inflictions. This was the golden age for fishermen, when fish were in universal demand, and gluts in the fish-market were unknown.

Strange to say, though Cabot and his English sailors discovered these rich fishing-grounds near Newfoundland, the people of England were not the first to turn them to profitable account. The French anticipated them. The boldest mariners and the most adventurous fishermen of those days were those of Brittany and Normandy. In their little cockle-shells of vessels they did not hesitate to sail away into these stormy seas. Seven years after Cabot's discovery—as early as 1504—they were fishing on these shores. They reached the Island of Cape Breton, and gave it the name it now bears, after their own home in Bretagne, or Brittany.

They were soon followed by the not less dauntless fishermen of the Basque Provinces, in the north-west of Spain. They have left a memorial of themselves in the name Port-au-Basques—a fine harbour, near Cape Ray, on the southern shore of Newfoundland, which is to become, this year, the terminus of the new line of railway, and the point of connection between Newfoundland and Canada. A few years ago a tombstone was found in Placentia bearing certain words which scholars have pronounced to be in the Basque language, so that some of them must have left their bones in the island. Portuguese and Spanish fishermen speedily followed, and these fisheries increased rapidly. There is no proof that any English fishermen took part in taking fish in these waters before 1517, and even then they must have been few, so slight are the traces of their presence. The total number of fishing-vessels in 1517 appears to have been about fifty, those carrying the flag of France being the most numerous. As early as 1522 some forty or fifty houses had been erected in Newfoundland for the temporary accommodation of the fishermen who resorted there in the summer. The English as yet had taken but a languid interest in these fisheries, though doubtless a few took part; and the reports they carried home of the vast shoals of fish soon stimulated others to follow. This has been denied recently, and an attempt has been made to show that the West-Country fishermen from the first embarked in large numbers in this enterprise, soon after the return of Cabot, and held on constantly and tenaciously. The statement rests on mere assumption, and is without substantial proof. Indeed, it is disproved by a letter written by John Rut, an English captain, to Henry VIII., and dated St. John's, August 3, 1527. He informs his sovereign, who had sent him and another captain to search for a north-west passage to India, that he found fishing in the harbour of St. John's eleven sail of Normans, one of Brittaine, and two Portuguese barques, but no English vessels; nor does he appear to have heard of any, although he sailed some hundreds of miles along the coast. The explanation of this is not far to seek. For many years previously the English had been extensively engaged in the Iceland fisheries, and being a conservative, practical people, and in the habit of selling goods in exchange for fish to the Icelanders, they, for a considerable time, neglected these new fisheries, and failed to appreciate their immense value; so that the Bretons, Normans, and Basques were grasping what the English had discovered.

This apathy, however, did not continue. Robert Thorne, in 1527, wrote to the English Government, urging them to vindicate their rights, but without effect. In 1536, however, we find Robert Hore, a wealthy merchant of London, at his own expense, attempting to found a colony in Newfoundland; but it ended in disastrous failure.

Meantime, however, the West-Country fishermen had learned of the success of their rivals, the French and Portuguese, and began to follow up these fisheries in increasing numbers. In 1578 there were four hundred vessels of various nationalities employed, but the majority were still French. The enthusiasm of the English, however, was now thoroughly awakened, and they speedily gained on their rivals; so that by the year 1600 there were two hundred vessels from the West-Country that every year went to Newfoundland, and employed as catchers on board, or curers on shore, over ten thousand men and boys. The fishery speedily became one of great national importance, and was considered worthy of legislative encouragement. Sir Walter Raleigh declared in the House of Commons that " it was the stay and support of the west counties of England." Sir William Monson, an Englishman, who wrote in 1610, declared that since the island was taken possession of, the fisheries had been worth £100,000 annually to British subjects—an immense sum in those days. He further said that these fisheries had greatly increased the number of England's ships and mariners. The fishing-fleet left England towards the middle or end of March for the fishing-grounds, and returned, bringing the products of their summer's fishing with them, in September. Not all of these hardy fishers from Devon and other Western counties who went out to Newfoundland, returned at the close of the fishing season. Some remained, and made homes for themselves in the new land. Year after year their numbers increased; and thus, by slow degrees, there grew up a resident population on the shores of the island. Though the fishery, for a long period, was mainly carried on from England, yet these sturdy settlers, in spite of every discouragement, held their ground, and at length grew up into a strong body of colonists, rooted in the soil, who carried on the fishery from the shores of the island, and, though sorely oppressed, stood up for their rights as freemen, and after a hard but bloodless battle, won the day. They formed the democracy—the "plebs"—the "bone and sinew"— who, for a century and a half, warred with the fishing patricians of the West Country, who wanted to keep them in serfdom. The battle of freedom, though on a small scale, was as nobly fought out here as in any other land, by determined, much-enduring men; and through toils and sufferings of no ordinary severity, they at length won their way to self-government, and the attainment of constitutional rights and liberties.

Newfoundland, therefore, is not a mere barren, fog-enveloped island, as most outsiders have long believed, where a few thousand fishermen secure a precarious existence by catching and curing cod. Its story is romantic, and connects itself with the history of both England and America at many points of deepest interest. In the New World the flag of England first waved here, and the first Colony was founded here. In prosecuting the fisheries of Newfoundland, English sailors first learned how to rule the waves. The attraction which first led Englishmen to these Western seas, and awoke in the national mind an impulse to colonize these new countries, was the immense fish-wealth in the seas around the island discovered by Cabot. The same holds good regarding France. Both France and England early engaged in the prosecution of the cod fisheries, and both drew from them enormous wealth, and thus increased their national greatness. The English and French fishermen engaged in these industries supplied the navy and commercial marine of both nations with bold and skilful sailors, and thus developed their sea-power. Both nations found here the best nurseries for their seamen; and to this day the French believe that the Newfoundland fisheries are essential to the supply of men for their navy, and sustain them by liberal bounties. Both nations were drawn to the region of the St. Lawrence, and were led to plant Colonies, originally with a view to carry on the fisheries and protect their interests. The rivalry between the two powers for obtaining the sovereignty of the soil arose in connection with the fisheries. The long wars between England and France, during the eighteenth century, were avowedly for the fisheries and the territories around them. Thus the fisheries of Newfoundland really laid the foundation of the Empire which England at length acquired in America, when, after a long contest with France, her supremacy was established, and her gallant Wolfe "died happy" on the Plains of Abraham. These fisheries were far more influential in bringing about the settlement of North America than all the gold of Mexico and Peru accomplished in that direction in Southern America. And thus the humble fishermen, who plied their hard labours along the shores and on the banks of Newfoundland and in the neighbouring seas, were the pioneers of the great host from the Old World, who in due time built up the United States, and created in modern days the great Dominion of Canada. They have done an honourable stroke of work in the great business of the world. England owes them much; and, in the case of her oldest Colony, much of that debt is still unpaid. Many of the wrongs and injuries of the past are still unredressed, and the obstructions to its prosperity, created by ill-advised Imperial Treaties, are still operative in the year of Her Majesty's Diamond Jubilee.

We have seen how tardy the English were in taking part in the fisheries of Newfoundland. For more than eighty years after the discovery of the island by Cabot it was the resort of fishermen of various nationalities, who used its shores for drying their fish. It was regarded as a sort of common property—"No Man's Land"—for England, though her fishermen used it, had never taken the trouble of claiming it as her own, or occupying it as part of her Empire. While France was ambitiously extending her domains and planting her colonists on the banks of the St. Lawrence, England had not got further than fishing on the shores of Newfoundland. In fact, it looked as if there were to be no English settlements in North America. Spain had got possession of all the southern part of the continent, and it seemed as though "New France" would absorb all the rest. Little was it anticipated then that a day would come when neither France nor Spain would own a foot of land on the whole continent of America, north and south; and when, of all the vast possessions of France, from the Gulf of St. Lawrence to the mouth of the Mississippi, her flag would wave over but two small islands—St. Pierre and Miquelon—at the mouth of Fortune Bay, Newfoundland.

STEADY BROOK FALLS.

ENGLAND'S OLDEST COLONY. 49

But "the spacious times of Great Elizabeth" at length dawned—the flowering-time of the English race—when mighty impulses were stirring the heart of the people, and the nation began to feel conscious of the great destiny that was awaiting it. It was the age of great statesmen, warriors, explorers, of fearless sea-rovers, of daring adventurers. It was an age of vast intellectual activity. The names of Bacon, Spenser, Shakespeare adorned its annals. Far-reaching projects for the extension of trade and commerce, for the acquisition of new territories beyond the seas, occupied men's minds. It was then that the thoughts of Englishmen began to turn once more to Cabot and his discoveries, made eighty-six years before, and now almost forgotten, but which had made Newfoundland and the mainland of North America theirs by right of discovery.

It was the year 1583. There was then living in England a brave patriotic nobleman named Sir Humphrey Gilbert—"one of the noblest spirits of the age," says Green, in his "History of the English People." Bancroft, the American historian, writes of him: "With a sounder judgment and a better knowledge" (than his contemporaries), "he watched the progress of the fisheries, and formed healthy plans for colonization. He had been a soldier and a member of Parliament. He was a judicious writer on navigation. He was one of those who alike despise fickleness and fear; danger never turned him aside from the pursuit of honour or the service of his sovereign, for he knew that death is inevitable and the fame of virtue immortal," as his own brave words expressed it;

E

"wherefore," he added, "in this behalf, *mutare vel timere sperno.*" His residence was Compton Castle, near Torbay, in Devonshire. He had a half-brother, also knighted by Elizabeth as Sir Walter Raleigh, whose fame was destined to be world-wide, and who, in a period more prolific of great men and great events than any other before or since, played a gallant part, and filled a large place in English history. As a soldier, Sir Humphrey Gilbert had won high distinction in his youth. In manhood he gave much attention to navigation, geography, and the great discoveries which were then going on in the Western hemisphere. He wrote a book, in which he tried to prove that it was possible to find a north-west passage to Eastern Asia. This far-seeing Devonshire knight had carefully studied these new fisheries in which so many of his countrymen were by this time engaged, and from whom, no doubt, he obtained his information regarding them. He held wider and truer views than any of his contemporaries on this subject, and considered that the right way to carry on these fisheries was by settling English people on the island, who could not only fish to greater advantage than on the migratory method then followed, but also cultivate the soil and make a home for themselves as well; while they added new territory to the realm. Besides, he thought it a shame that his countrymen should be content to look on with indifference, while French and Spaniards were dividing among themselves the soil and riches of the New World. He knew what rights England had acquired by Cabot's discovery, and he believed that it was her duty to do her part in exploring and settling these new countries, and thus open a field for the enterprise of her people. He took counsel with his step-brother, Sir Walter Raleigh, who held similar views, and together they laid the matter before Queen Elizabeth. That far-seeing sovereign at once adopted and sanctioned their project, and gave Gilbert the first charter that passed the great seal of England for colonization in America. Its terms were of the most liberal description. Bancroft defined it as follows: "To the people who might belong to his colony *the rights of Englishmen were promised.* To Gilbert, the possession for himself or his assigns of the soil which he might discover, and the sole jurisdiction, both civil and criminal, of the territory within two hundred leagues of his settlement, with supreme executive and legislative authority." It was a sufficiently generous patent so far as the leader of the expedition was concerned, as it conferred on him every power and privilege, but placed the settlers under the irresponsible rule of one man or one corporation. In those despotic days individual liberty was of small account.

A little squadron of five small vessels was collected. On the eve of his departure he received from Elizabeth a golden anchor guided by a lady, a token of the Queen's regard. The touching story of this enterprise and its tragic termination has been often told, and need not be repeated except in a few brief words. He reached the harbour of St. John's safely with four of his ships. There he found thirty-four vessels engaged in fishing—nearly half of them English. On the 5th of August, 1583, he and his officers and men landed. The captains and crews of the fishing-vessels were summoned to attend. In the midst of the motley assemblage, composed of French, Portuguese, Spaniards, and English, the Devon knight stood up and read his patent authorizing him to take possession of the island on behalf of his royal mistress. The usual feudal ceremonies were gone through; the banner of England was hoisted on a flagstaff, and the arms of England affixed to a wooden pillar; and Newfoundland was solemnly declared to be a portion of the British Empire.

The sequel of the story is sad enough. How with three of his ships he sailed south to make further discoveries; how one was wrecked, and the winter coming on, and his provisions running short, he was forced to shape his course for England; and how he was overtaken by a tempest, and the little *Squirrel*, of ten tons, with Sir Humphrey Gilbert and all on board, sank amid the dark billows of the Atlantic. It was a tragic death, but the death of a hero; for that scene amid the pitiless waves is brightened for a moment, as by the lightning's flash, and we see him seated on the deck, tranquil and fearless, the Book in his hand; and as the other ship came within hail, those on board could hear his strong voice, full of cheerful courage, ringing out those memorable words across the angry billows, "Courage, my lads! we are as near heaven by sea as by land"—words to which every brave heart will respond for evermore. And thus Sir Humphrey Gilbert, scholar, soldier, discoverer, philosopher, and colonizer, heroic and pious in life and in death, was seen no more amid the struggles and turmoils of men.

The first attempt to colonize Newfoundland ended thus disastrously, as, indeed, did most of the first efforts at planting Colonies in the Western hemisphere. To Newfoundland the loss of Sir Humphrey Gilbert was great and irreparable. Had he lived and succeeded in planting a Colony, the cultivation of the soil would have gone on hand in hand with the fisheries. The interior would have been opened up and turned to account; and the wealth derived from the fisheries would have remained in the island for the development of its natural resources, which time has since proved to be abundant. A prosperous resident population would thus have grown up. Instead of this, Gilbert's plans were set aside. The country fell into the hands of West-Country fishing adventurers, who exploited the fisheries for their own benefit, and forming, as they did, a wealthy and powerful corporation, greedy and unscrupulous, they were able to get laws passed which secured them a monopoly of the fisheries, which they carried on from England, and prohibited fishermen from settling in the island or erecting houses. All had to return home at the close of the fishing season. For the benefit of a few greedy, selfish men, the island was kept for a long time a mere fishing station, and all the money made by fishing was spent in other lands, and the country remained in a wilderness condition. On what small things do the destinies of men turn! Had Gilbert survived that Atlantic storm, the history of

Newfoundland might have been very different from that actually recorded. But his failure to colonize stirred up others to similar efforts, and led the way to the development of the New England Colonies. Newfoundlanders have reason to revere his name and memory. It is humiliating, in these days, to find any one attempting to belittle the gallant knight of Devon, and detract from the glory he so well merited.

The reign of Elizabeth thus witnessed the first attempt by Englishmen at planting Colonies. Three hundred years rolled away, and a greater than Elizabeth now occupies the throne of a far mightier Empire than that over which Elizabeth swayed the sceptre. The greatness of Elizabeth none will question. Her genius for governing, her marvellous insight into men and events, her piercing intellect, have rarely been surpassed; but these mental powers were united to a diamond heart that was seldom touched by pity or sympathy, and never expended itself in relieving human woes, or on plans for promoting human happiness. She lived in lonely isolation—powerful, ambitious, proud, unscrupulous, and selfish. Her age, no doubt, was marked by great men and great events, but it had little of the moral glory that distinguishes the reign of Victoria, whom her people delight to call "the Good," and who is enshrined in the hearts of her subjects. She, too, possesses all the mental powers that distinguish a great ruler; but she adds to these all the moral qualities that awaken our love and reverence. Her era far surpasses that of Elizabeth in all that is comprehended under the name of

Progress. "Nobler manners, purer laws," vast strides in science, in art, in literature, in discoveries and inventions that benefit and bless her people, have marked her reign. The Victorian age has never been equalled in the past, whatever the future may hold in store.

One feature of that age, specially noteworthy, has been the vast expansion of the Colonies of the Empire. Elizabeth's reign saw the commencement of them, and Queen Victoria's accession to the throne was marked by an important advance in the method of governing the Colonies, which has bound them more closely to the mother-land than any former policy. Then began the extension of free institutions, the gift of self-governing powers to the Colonies, which have enabled them to shape their own destinies and develop their own resources, and fitted them for final incorporation as members of the Empire. England's oldest Colony has shared in this great boon of self-government; and, in common with the others, has profited thereby. It is the aim of the writer of this little volume to describe its condition, and, if possible, throw some light upon its prospects in the future.

CHAPTER IV.

The Makers and Making of Newfoundland—Abortive attempts at Colonizing—The Fishermen the real Colonizers—Monopoly of West-Country Adventurers—Its Growth and Extent—Tyranny by Act of Parliament—The Fishing Admirals—Struggles of the Resident Population for Freedom—Dawn after Darkness—First Governor—Liberty slowly won against heavy odds—Wrongs of the Colony—Progress of Newfoundland in the Reign of Queen Victoria.

THE failure of Sir Humphrey Gilbert's expedition had such a discouraging effect, that for twenty-seven years no fresh attempt was made to found a Colony in the island. Still his effort was far from being fruitless. The bold undertaking, so well conceived, so bravely carried out, and so tragic in its termination, fixed the attention of Englishmen on Newfoundland and its fisheries as nothing else could have done. The heroic Gilbert did not die in vain. His attempt at colonization—the first yet made—awoke in the minds of his countrymen that spirit of adventure which led them to plant Colonies in New England which in due time became the Great Republic of the West. The very next year after Gilbert's death, his half-brother, Sir Walter Raleigh, founded a Colony, under a patent from Queen Elizabeth, which he named Virginia, after the maiden queen; and as no other Colony can claim to date so far back (1584), it has been usually designated "The Old Dominion." But neither was this attempt successful at first; and it was thirteen years afterwards that the first permanent English Colony in Virginia was planted on the shores of Chesapeake Bay, in 1620.

But Newfoundland was now prominently before the eyes of Englishmen, and ere long renewed attempts at colonization were made. The fisheries were rapidly extending and pouring wealth into the western counties of England. To persons of broad and liberal views it became clear that time and money were wasted in carrying on the fisheries from England, and that the right method was to hold out inducements to fishermen to live permanently near the fishing-grounds, and at the same time cultivate the soil and make homes for themselves. These views were strongly urged in a pamphlet published by John Guy, a merchant, and afterwards mayor of Bristol, in 1609. This publication made such a deep impression on the public mind that a company was formed to carry out the enterprise it suggested. Several noblemen having influence at the Court of James I. took part in the undertaking. The most illustrious name on the roll of this company was that of Lord Bacon, the apostle of experimental philosophy. The importance of Newfoundland as a site for an English Colony did not escape his wide-ranging eye, and his sagacity may be judged of by one of his memorable sayings, often quoted since, that "its fisheries were more valuable than all the mines of Peru"—a judgment which time has amply verified.

With Bacon were associated in this enterprise the Earl of Southampton (Lord Keeper), Sir Daniel Doun, Sir Percival Willoughby, John Guy, the wealthy merchant, and several other gentlemen of good repute and position. Guy was appointed Governor of the proposed Colony, and came out with a body of settlers; but this attempt also proved a failure.

Then came, in 1615, Captain Richard Whitbourne, mariner, of Exmouth, Devonshire, a noteworthy character in English maritime history. He received a commission from the Admiralty of England to proceed to Newfoundland for the purpose of establishing order among the fishing population, and remedying certain abuses which had grown up. He acquitted himself of the task admirably. He knew the country well, having spent forty years in trading to Newfoundland, and formed a sort of romantic attachment to the island. He could fight a ship as well as sail one. When the Spanish Armada invaded England, Captain Whitbourne fitted out a vessel, at his own expense, for the defence of his native land. He was one of Elizabeth's gallant band of Devon captains who dashed out of Torbay into the very midst of the Spanish galleons as they passed. When, in his old age, he retired from active life, he wrote an account of the island he loved so well, entitled, "A Discourse and Discovery of Newfoundland," with the view of inducing Englishmen to settle there. In this book he spoke highly of the climate, soil, fisheries, and other resources of the island; and it is a remarkable fact that now, in the reign of Queen Victoria, when roads and railways have opened up the interior, and a geological survey has made known its agricultural, mineral, and lumbering capabilities, the representations of the ancient mariner, made two hundred and seventy years ago, have been confirmed in a remarkable degree. King James I. thought so highly of the book that he ordered a copy to be sent to every parish in the kingdom. The Archbishops of Canterbury and York issued a letter recommending it to the notice of the people, in order to induce Englishmen to settle in Newfoundland. Thus two hundred and seventy years ago Newfoundland was a name frequently on the lips of Englishmen, and it was probably more widely known among them than it came to be long afterwards, when it was misrepresented and decried by selfish, greedy, fishing adventurers, who wanted to monopolize its fisheries. Newfoundland has reason to remember the Devonshire captain with gratitude. Within the last few years the first real inland town which has sprung up on the new line of railway was named Whitbourne, after the gallant old sailor. It has a beautiful site, and is likely to grow steadily.

The next attempt at colonization was by Sir George Calvert, afterwards Lord Baltimore, in 1623. He was a man of intelligence, lofty integrity, and great capacity for business. He built a fine mansion at Ferryland, forty miles south of St. John's. He carefully selected settlers of a superior type, and spent £30,000 on his settlement—an immense sum in those days. But the site of his Colony was not well chosen, and the continuous attacks of the French, who were trying to establish themselves in Newfoundland, so harassed him that he became disheartened and returned to England; but nearly all the colonists he brought with him remained to increase the resident population.

Sir David Kirke, a brave sea-captain, who had won high honours in warlike operations against the French in Canada, succeeded Lord Baltimore at Ferryland, and used every effort to promote the settlement of the country, and not without a considerable measure of success. He died at Ferryland in 1655.

These organized attempts, under royal sanction, to colonize the island were attended with but a scanty measure of success. It was not by these that settlement was to be effected, but by the hardy fishermen themselves, who year after year, and in spite of all efforts to drive them out, established themselves along the shores of the island and erected hamlets and villages. In the midst of so many difficulties and discouragements as they had to encounter the process proved to be very slow, and the Colony did not advance at the same rate as the other American Colonies founded at a later date. Seventy-one years after the arrival of Sir Humphrey Gilbert the island contained a resident population of only 350 families, or about 1750 persons. These were distributed in fifteen small settlements along the eastern shore. The principal of them were Torbay, Quidi Vidi, St. John's, Bay of Bulls, Ferryland, Renewse, Aquaforte. Twenty years later, in 1680, the population was 2280. In 1698 they numbered only 2640. Even St. John's, the capital, increased very slowly, and in 1780 had only 1605 inhabitants.

It must be remembered, however, that in addition to these there was a large floating population of many thousands, who frequented the shores during summer to carry on the fisheries, but left for their homes in England on the approach of winter. Even in Captain Whitbourne's day the trade and fisheries of the island were largely in the hands of the English, as his appointment shows, for he could not have exercised jurisdiction except over British subjects. He heard complaints of no less than one hundred and seventy masters of English vessels, regarding injuries to the trade and fisheries; and he found that there were, besides the vessels of foreign flags, two hundred and fifty English ships employed in the fisheries. In 1626 Devonshire alone sent one hundred and fifty vessels to the cod-fishery.

The question, then, presents itself, Why was the settlement of the island so slow? The climate was healthy, the soil amply repaid cultivation, the fisheries were most productive. Out of the many thousands who resorted to it in the fishing season, how was it so few took up their permanent abode in the island?

There was a sufficient reason for this, which we must now very briefly explain. It was owing to the operation of one of the most nefarious and heartless systems, continued for over one hundred and fifty years, that the brain of man ever devised to keep a fine island, one-sixth larger than Ireland, in a wilderness condition, and to forcibly prevent its settlement, in order that a few West-Country "merchant adventurers" might enrich themselves by the exclusive use of its shores and fisheries. Never was a Colony so cruelly and unjustly dealt with. That successive British Governments sanctioned and sustained the plans and operations of these selfish, greedy cormorants is matter of astonishment, and far from creditable to the statesmen who then guided the policy of the Empire.

It must be understood that at this time, so far as the English were concerned, the fisheries had been carried on by merchants, shipowners, and traders, who resided in the West of England, some of them in London. They sent out their ships and hired fishing-crews to Newfoundland early in the summer. The fish caught were salted and dried ashore. When winter approached the fishermen took their departure for England, carrying with them whatever portion of the fish had not been previously shipped for foreign markets. These "merchant adventurers," as they were called, found that it was for their interest to discourage the settlement of the country, as they wished to retain its harbours, and coves, and fishing-grounds for the use of their own captains and servants while engaged in catching and curing fish. They got at length to regard the island as a snug preserve for their exclusive use, and that any one who settled there was an interloper who should be driven away. They coolly wanted to prevent the occupation of an island, containing forty-two thousand square miles, by any permanent settlers, in order that they might use the shores for drying their fish, and enjoy, in their own country, the riches thus gathered.

But, in spite of all their efforts, a few hardy and adventurous persons began to form little settlements along the shore. The island had strong attractions for them, and they saw that they could make comfortable homes for themselves, and combine the cultivation of the soil with fishing. The fishing merchants and ship-owners took the alarm, and went to war with these settlers who had come out from England as fishermen in the merchants' ships, and as part of their crews. They were determined to root them out, or at all events to keep their numbers as small as possible. Being men of wealth and position, they had great influence at Court and with successive English Governments of those days, while the poor fishing settlers were of small account, and their case could obtain no hearing. The capitalists were able to persuade the English statesmen, and even the people, that the fisheries would be ruined if a resident population should be allowed to grow up in the island, and that they would no longer be a nursery of seamen for the navy. Further, they misled the public by representing the island as hopelessly barren, and, in regard to its soil and climate, utterly unfit for human habitation. They pictured the interior, though no one had ever seen it, as alternations of naked rocks, swamps, and bogs, in which no tree would grow, and no vegetable soil existed.

They had no great trouble in persuading the English Governments to enact unjust and injurious laws to prevent the settlement of the island, and to keep it for ever in the degraded condition of a stage for drying fish. These laws forbade any one going to Newfoundland as a settler, and ordained that all fishermen should return to England at the close of each fishing season. Masters of vessels were compelled to give bonds of one hundred pounds binding them to bring back each year such persons as they took out. Settlement within six miles of the coast was prohibited under heavy penalties. No one could cultivate or enclose the smallest piece of ground, or even repair a house without licence, which was rarely granted. This oppressive policy was maintained for more than a hundred years, and sufficiently explains why the population increased so slowly, and why the Colony made little or no progress in the arts and appliances of civilized life.

Strange to say, notwithstanding all these hardships and repressive measures, the sturdy settlers held their ground, and slowly and steadily increased in numbers. Between them and their oppressors a bitter antagonism, and in some instances a fierce animosity, sprang up; and it is not wonderful that it should be so. The settlers found themselves deprived of all civil rights and legal protection, at the mercy of a set of absentee proprietors, who prohibited them from using or owning the land, and even from utilizing the harbours, till their own retainers were provided for. Still the battle went on. There must have been among these settlers a strong, manly, independent spirit. Had there not been among them men possessing much vigour of character and solid worth, they could not have carried on the contest so bravely against the myrmidons of their wealthy oppressors, and at last conquered them, and won their freedom.

RATTLING BROOK, EXPLOITS RIVER.

It reminds one forcibly of the contest between the patricians and plebeians, in the early days of Rome, after the ejection of the kings—a contest of right against might—which went on for two hundred years, and ended in the victory of the plebeians. The latter endured terrible miseries and hardships—they were denied their share of the public lands, and of all part in the government; they became debtors and serfs to the patricians, just like the poor Newfoundland fishermen to their oppressors. Still they held on and gained their rights step by step—got their tribunes to protect them—their decemviri and agrarian laws, and at last became eligible to the consulship. The patricians fought desperately for two centuries to prevent all this, but in the end were beaten, and had to admit the plebeians to a fair share in the government of the State, just as here in Newfoundland the democracy won their rights. And there is another point of resemblance. The whole contest in Rome was a bloodless one. There were no tumults or riots—no revolutions. Both parties were possessed of self-control, and obeyed the laws till they were altered. So here—the settlers, though sorely wronged, never had recourse to violence. They bore their lot patiently, and sought their rights by constitutional methods, and finally conquered. Still the the conflict was very trying, and the sufferings of men who were kept outside the pale of law, and without any civilizing influences, were intense.

When the merchant adventurers found that the settlers were increasing notwithstanding all their repressive efforts, they applied, in 1670, to the Lords of Trade and Plantations, and declared that unless the settlers were removed the fisheries would be destroyed, and the English navy deprived of its supply of seamen. It seems almost incredible, but it is true, that these Lords sent out Sir John Berry, a naval officer, with orders to drive out the resident fishermen and burn their dwellings. This barbarous edict was not revoked for six years, and what cruelties were wrought under it will never be known. There is, however, reason to believe that Sir John Berry was a humane man, and did not strictly carry out his orders. The climax of repression was reached when a certain Major Elford, lieutenant-governor at St. John's, very strongly urged the ministers of the day "to allow no woman to land in the island, and also that means should be adopted to remove those that were there." This was indeed going to the root of the matter, but it does not appear that any one tried to carry out this sweeping proposal. The deportation of the women would have been a difficult task.

In point of fact, these Newfoundland patricians were many degrees more thorough-going and unscrupulous than their Roman prototypes. They got the Star Chamber of Charles I. to issue an enactment that if a person in Newfoundland killed another, or stole the value of forty shillings, the offender was to be sent to England, and on conviction of either offence, to be hanged. Another law promulgated by this notorious Chamber was that the master of the first ship entering a harbour was to be admiral for the season and magistrate for the district, with unlimited power to decide all questions regarding property and all other disputes. Thus arose the government by "Fishing Admirals," as they were named—perhaps the most absurd and tyrannical pretence at the administration of justice ever devised by the ingenuity of man. Strange as it may sound, in 1698, in the reign of that liberal sovereign William III., the British Parliament passed an Act, at the request of the patrician monopolists, confirming and extending this preposterous arrangement. This unfortunate statute of William for a very long period obstructed all improvement in the country. It ordained that the master of a vessel arriving first in a harbour was to be admiral for the season, and was allowed to take as much of the beach as he chose for his own use. The masters of the second and third vessels arriving at the same harbour were to be vice-admiral and rear-admiral, with similar privileges. When these worthies had helped themselves, if anything was left, the unfortunate fishermen might obtain a scrap. No attention was paid to the qualifications of these Fishing Admirals. The first rude, ignorant skipper who made a short passage was absolute ruler for the season. They were the servants of the merchant adventurers, and therefore personally interested in questions of property that arose, and as one of them naïvely remarked, "it would be strange if they did not do justice to themselves." They were the enemies of the poor residents, whom they wanted to trample out.

The triumph of the merchants over their fellow-subjects in this lone isle was now as complete as that of a warrior who storms a city. Their servants, the

Fishing Admirals, took possession of the best fishing-stations, drove out the inhabitants from their own houses when they chose, and seized their gardens and fishing-grounds. In determining cases they took bribes without any pretence at concealment, and carried on, for many long years, a system of robbery and oppression. All accounts agree in representing them as at once knaves and tyrants, though doubtless there were individual exceptions.

In vain did the resident people, groaning under the lash of these petty tyrants, petition the Lords of Trade and lay before them their grievances. The wealthy merchants were able to get their petitions thrown aside with contempt. Again and again they asked for the appointment of a Governor to regulate the affairs of the island. That, above all, was a measure the merchants and ship-owners dreaded. It might disturb their pleasant monopoly and weaken their control. A Governor might take the part of the settlers, and they fiercely resisted his appointment. What they wanted was, as one of their own party expressed it, "that Newfoundland should always be considered as a great English ship moored near the Banks, during the fishing season, for the convenience of English fishermen, the people being subject to naval laws and regulations."

During this hard struggle the lot of these poor fishermen must have been very bitter, and the miseries they endured terrible. It is not wonderful that many of them became utterly discouraged and escaped to America, and there aided materially in building up the New England fisheries. In their little wooden hamlets sprinkled around the sea-margin their outlook was dreary enough. They could earn but a bare subsistence. They had no schools for their children, no ministers of religion among them. All around were the dense woods extending to the seashore, no roads, and only a few paths cut through them. Before them was the great ocean from which alone they were permitted to draw their means of subsistence. Their treatment was so harsh that if in these days the inmates of a prison or a workhouse were dealt with in like fashion, the public indignation would be loud and deep. How could they advance in the arts of civilized life, or improve their adopted country?

It is marvellous to find that they still held on and never gave way to despair; resisted their foes by patient constitutional measures and by petitioning to have their wrongs righted. They were conscious of having right on their side, and had faith that it would win the day in the long run.

Their courage and patience were at last rewarded. A day of deliverance began to dawn. The Government and people of England at length found out that they had been deceived, both in regard to the country and the character of its fisheries, and that the notion of their being "a nursery for sailors to man the royal navy" was a snare and a delusion. Restrictions on the settlement of the country were very slowly and cautiously removed, one after another. The obnoxious statute of William III., however, was left still unrepealed; and retarded all improvements. The change for the better was brought about by the commodores and captains of the royal ships which were periodically appointed to this station. They saw the terrible injustice which was inflicted on a patient and inoffensive people. One of them, named Lord Vere Beauclerk, a clear-headed, benevolent nobleman, made such strong representations to the Board of Trade that the British Government were induced to appoint Captain Henry Osborne, in 1729, to be the first Governor of Newfoundland. This constituted a new era in the history of the Colony, and pioneered the way for all the reforms which followed. It was a practical recognition of Newfoundland as a Colony of the Empire, and no longer a mere fishing-station. This rendered all sorts of improvements possibilities in the future.

But a long and weary struggle for constitutional freedom and civil rights had yet to follow. In fact, it was not till about eighty years ago that the last of these unjust laws was repealed, and people were allowed to possess lands and build houses, and take some steps towards self-government. In fact, the reign of the Fishing Admirals did not end for nearly another half-century, owing to the pertinacity with which the monopolists resisted the action of the new method of naval government under admirals and captains of the British Navy, which, though not the most desirable way of governing a colony, was a great improvement on anything yet enjoyed. It prepared the way for local civil government, and finally for political freedom. In 1729, when the first Governor arrived, the resident population had grown to be six thousand strong.

ENGLAND'S OLDEST COLONY. 71

To recount the events which followed in the struggle for freedom would be to write the history of Newfoundland, and that does not enter into the scope of the present volume, which is limited to giving some account of the condition of the Colony in the present year of our beloved Queen's Diamond Jubilee. The author has previously told the story of the Colony in his "Newfoundland, the oldest British Colony," and in the "Text-Book of Newfoundland History," to which the reader is referred for fuller information.

It must suffice to mention that, although the sufferings of the people were mitigated, they were by no means ended. It was no longer illegal to settle in the country, but still no permission was yet given to cultivate the soil, and no stage could be erected for handling fish, by the residents, till their lords and masters from England were satisfied. During so many years of oppression the fishermen had become so poor that they had to obtain advances in provisions and clothing at the commencement of each fishing season, at high prices, and at the close to pay for them in fish, the price of which was fixed by the supplier. Thus arose the "supplying," or "credit system," which kept the fishermen constantly in debt and dependent on the capitalist, and in the end caused innumerable evils. Still slowly and step by step improvements came. The resident population increased in numbers and influence. The navigation laws were extended to the Colony. A Supreme Court for the administration of justice, presided over by a Chief Justice and two assistant judges, was established in 1793. Freedom of worship and complete religious toleration were granted, by which a deplorable system of religious persecution was ended for ever. Still the advance was slow, as may be judged by the fact that, as late as 1799, houses erected in St. John's without a licence were pulled down by order of the Governor; and restrictions on building, and on enclosing and cultivating the ground, were not entirely abolished till 1820. The first road was made in 1825. In 1832 the great boon of Representative Government was granted, and in 1854 this concession was enlarged and completed by the grant of Responsible Government. In 1834 the resident population was found to be seventy-five thousand; and the population of St. John's was fifteen thousand.

The victory was complete all along the line. The battle for freedom was won against heavy odds. We cannot withhold our admiration from a people who displayed such patient fortitude amid sore sufferings and hardships. There must have been among them many a "Village Hampden," who on this obscure stage confronted tyranny with "dauntless breast." It was Englishmen against Englishmen. It was the proud, domineering aristocracy of the West Country on the one side, with their followers, and the plucky, stubborn democracy, whose ancestors had been born on the same soil, on the other side. But the latter were powerfully aided by a gallant contingent from the Emerald Isle, who had, year after year, arrived, and in spite of all opposition, established themselves in the new land. During the troublous times in Ireland they had fled from oppression, and found new homes beyond the

Western waves. They came at length to be about equal in numbers to the settlers from England. In the battle for freedom they were sure to be on the right side; and in the long struggle for civil and religious liberty and political rights they and their leaders played no insignificant part. In fact, in the final struggle they led the van.

True to their traditions, however, the "merchant adventurers" fought desperately against every innovation that threatened the old order of things, and resisted every amelioration of the social and political condition of the people. They protested against the appointment of a Governor; they supported the rule of the Fishing Admirals; they frantically resisted the introduction of courts of law and magistrates. Above all, they concentrated their forces against Representative and Responsible Government. In later years their followers and supporters here fiercely opposed the introduction of railways, or any other way of opening up the interior and turning to account the rich natural resources of the country. They wanted the people to be chained down to the fisheries, of which they were to be lords and masters. But the plucky plebs met and overthrew them at all points; and now many of their modern representatives have renounced their antiquated creed, and joined the party of progress, being convinced that old feuds should be forgotten, and all join hand-in-hand for the improvement of a country whose progress has been so unworthily retarded, but which will yet be a bright gem in the colonial Empire of Great Britain.

We have seen that the Imperial Mother, deceived and misled by the selfish adventurers, dealt hardly and harshly with her eldest-born Colony; and, by unjust and cruel laws, sustained the tyrants for more than a century and a half. No other British Colony met with such harsh treatment. When Lord Salisbury described it in euphonious terms as having been "the sport of historic misfortunes," he would have been nearer the mark had he said "the victim of historic wrongs and cruelties." For not only did England back the oppressors, but, worse still, she formed treaties with the French, by which the best half of their island home was torn from the people, and virtually given over to another nation. These French shore-treaties, as we shall see farther on in this volume, have done more than all other causes combined to retard the progress of the country. Fishing privileges given to the French by the Imperial Treaties have been the means of excluding the people of Newfoundland from settling on the best portion of the island; while the concession of St. Pierre and Miquelon has given enormous advantages to our French rivals, which, having been supplemented by their bounties, threaten the prosperity of our fisheries. To crown all, St. Pierre and Miquelon have become smuggling depôts by which our revenue has suffered, and many of our people become demoralized by the temptations held out to engage in smuggling practices. It is surely time that the brave and generous people of England looked these facts in the face, and took into consideration the wrongs of the past which have been met by unswerving and devoted loyalty on the part of her eldest-born Colony. Some atonement for that past is surely called for, and some help to remove existing evils that still sorely hamper the Colony's progress.

The natural capabilities of the country and the spirit of its people may be judged of by the substantial progress made since the removal of restrictions and the grant of self-government. Contrast the Newfoundland of the past, with its Fishing Admirals and the serfdom of its people, with Newfoundland in this year of Her Majesty's Diamond Jubilee. The whistle of the locomotive is heard in the solitudes of the interior, where the deer, the wolf, and the fox were once the undisturbed proprietors. Seven hundred miles of railway now traverse the island, and ere the year closes a steam ferry will connect the island with Canada. Instead of bog, rock, and marsh, as the monopolists represented, the interior is proved to contain magnificent stretches of fertile land and rich forests; coal beds and mineral deposits of immense value. Already the copper mines of the north have yielded ten million dollars' worth of ore, and one iron pyrites mine on Pilley's Island has shipped ore to the value of nearly a million dollars. One of the most valuable iron mines in the world has been recently opened near St. John's. Asbestos has been discovered in numerous localities, and borings for petroleum have been successful. Lumbering is active; agricultural products already average the value of seven hundred and fifty thousand dollars annually. The Atlantic cable finds a resting-place on the shores of the island, and numerous land-lines connect the exterior districts with the capital. There is direct steam communication with England and America. All this is mainly the result of some forty years of progress. The revenue has risen to one million six hundred thousand dollars per annum. The population has increased to two hundred and ten thousand. The misfortunes of fires in the capital and a severe financial crisis have been met by a spirited people and surmounted. The island now presents an inviting field for capital and enterprise. Such is Newfoundland's record of progress during the reign of Queen Victoria.

CHAPTER V.

Evolution of the Railway in Newfoundland—Pioneer Road-making seventy years ago—Inception of a Railway—Sir William Whiteway, the Railway Leader—Opposition to the Project—Story of the Construction of the Great Northern and Western Railway—R. G. Reid, Esq., Contractor—Resources of the Country opened up—Character of the Contract—Advantages to the Colony—Settlement on Lands—Forests and Mineral riches—Will the Railway be Remunerative?

For more than two hundred and fifty years after the occupation of the island by the English no roads were constructed. Intercourse between the fishing-settlements sprinkled around the coast was maintained by sea, or by rough paths cut through the woods. The first step in civilization—the construction of roads—had not yet been taken. This was a result of the old theory, that the island was to be a fishing-station and nothing more. It was held that for fishermen the natural and proper highway was the sea, and such a luxury as a road quite unnecessary, if not demoralizing, as it might distract their attention from their proper occupation. But a daring innovator, in the person of Sir Thomas Cochrane, arrived as Governor, and to the horror and disgust of the fishery patricians, he entered on road-making, and constructed nearly twenty miles of roads of a cheap description to some of the villages in the neighbourhood of the capital. This was done only seventy years ago. The people were delighted. They had no idea till then what a pleasant and useful thing a road was, and some of them began to clear lands and settle themselves in neat comfortable farmhouses along these lines of road, and to raise crops and feed cattle. It was quite a new era. When, a few years after, the people obtained Representative Government, they insisted that an annual grant for building and repairing roads should be voted out of the revenue. Road-making went on rapidly. One road, eighty miles in length, was constructed from St. John's to Placentia, the old French capital, and many others in various directions. The people began to discover that the nearer portion of the interior, at all events, was not a dreary morass, but contained excellent land and pleasant sites for farms. By the year 1870 there were one thousand miles of postal roads constructed, and two thousand miles of district roads connecting with these.

One innovation is sure to introduce others. The ideas of the people began to expand, and ere long they discovered what great possibilities their country presented. These roads traversed only a narrow margin within a few miles of the salt water, and connected together the various fishing towns and villages. But now the people began to ask, " What about the interior of this great island, containing forty-two thousand square miles, of which we know little or nothing ? Is it not possible to turn this huge territory to profitable account?" Such questions were emphasized by the fact that the population was increasing rapidly, at the rate of twenty-two per cent. each decade, whilst the fisheries, which furnished their main source of subsistence, were stationary, and in some places declining. No wonder that it should be asked, Is this vast interior to remain for ever an unpeopled wilderness? and are the people to be cooped up to starve along the sea-margin?

By some fortunate chance, in 1864, a geological survey, under the direction of Alexander Murray, F.G.S., an eminent geologist, had been appointed, and the annual reports of the scientific officials who conducted it began to tell of vast stretches of good lands in the interior, well adapted for settlement, amounting in the aggregate to several millions of acres, of magnificent pine forests, of mineral deposits, of extensive coal beds. These reports were at first received with derisive incredulity by all but a few. When, however, in 1864, a rich copper mine was opened at Tilt Cove, and was speedily followed by the discovery and working of two others, the doubters and scoffers were partially silenced; and they were forced to admit that, after all, there might be something in the interior worth looking after, if only you could get at it.

It was at this stage that the idea of a railway began to float dimly before the minds of some of the more thoughtful and intelligent; but it was at first spoken of with bated breath, lest advocacy might expose the bold innovators to the suspicion of insanity. By the great mass of the people the project of building a railway was regarded as entirely beyond the means of the Colony. Timid, short-sighted people declared it would bring no returns—"would not pay for the grease of wheels," as a sturdy old fishery notable expressed it—and that the end would be ruin and universal bankruptcy. The old opponents of change and progress regarded the building of a railway with horror. The opposition to it was formidable—all but overwhelming.

Sir William Whiteway was at this time (1875) Solicitor-General of the Colony and a member of the Cabinet. He became convinced that there was only one way of securing a prosperous future for the Colony, and providing for the wants of an increasing population—namely, to open the interior by a railway, so as to turn to account its natural resources, which he believed to be rich and abundant. His first act was, in the face of a strong opposition, among whom were members of the Cabinet, to obtain from the Legislature a grant for a survey through the island to Bay St. George, in order to determine what facilities for railway construction it presented. This survey was carried out under the direction of Mr. Sandford, C.E., of Canada. It was not, however, till 1878, when Sir William became Premier, that he was able to push forward his project. The construction of a transinsular railway, in addition to immediate advantages, he saw would in the future lead to a colonization of the interior, and the extension of farming, lumbering, and mining. Looking further, he saw that by such a line facilities of communication with the continent would

TOAD'S COVE.

be greatly increased, trade enlarged, and many commercial and social advantages secured, so that, should the people desire it, union with the Dominion of Canada would ultimately become attainable. Having arrived at these conclusions, Sir William, on becoming Premier, adopted railway building as the main feature of his policy, and on it he risked his own political future and that of his party. From this course he has never swerved for twenty years. He faced courageously a powerful opposition at first, which was not confined to the ranks of his political opponents, but numbered members of his own party. With a tenacity of purpose that braved all risks, he continued his advocacy of the railway policy, threw himself on the support of the people, and now he has the satisfaction of seeing his statesmanlike project crowned with success. This Jubilee Year will witness the completion of the transinsular railway, five hundred and fifty miles in length, by which Newfoundland and Canada will be brought within six hours of steaming. The first sod of the first railway line was turned in 1881, and now there are nearly seven hundred miles of railway, all the property of the Colony. Sir William Whiteway's name will be for ever associated with the introduction of a railway system. He had able co-workers, such as Sir Ambrose Shea, Mr. A. W. Harvey, Mr. A. M. Mackay, Mr. J. J. Little, and others, who stood by him in the conflict; but to him must be accorded the distinction of being leader in a movement which has introduced a new order of affairs, and started the Colony on the path of progress. That Sir William has the great majority of the people with him in his railway policy is proved by the fact that he has been for nineteen years a member of the Executive Council or Government, during fifteen of which he was Premier —a position which he fills at present.

To people resident in densely-inhabited countries it might appear almost an act of insanity to build a railway right through an uninhabited country. They would naturally say, settle the country first; extend common roads through it; and then, when a sufficient population has occupied it, you will be warranted in building a railway for their accommodation that will be sure to pay. But that is not the accepted doctrine on the western side of the Atlantic. There the practice is to run a railway through the uninhabited country at first, in order to have it rapidly settled. The other method would be far too slow, and would not work in practice. Emigration follows the line of railway. From the trunk line branch lines are built in all directions, as settlement advances, and towns and villages spring up. Common roads radiate from the main line where a railway would be too costly. Of course, such railways for a time—perhaps a long time— do not pay working expenses even. But indirectly they far more than repay their cost by immensely enhancing the value of the lands they open up; by increasing the productiveness of the soil and the number of the inhabitants, whose contributions swell the public revenue, and whose industry adds to the wealth of the country. In this way the State finds it most advantageous to borrow money for the construction of railways, paying for a time interest, as well as working expenses in part. The revenue from such lines of railway increases steadily as settlement advances, and in the end the gain to the State, directly and indirectly, is enormous.

The State may either build and own the line of railway, or, what is more usual, it may contract with a company for the construction, giving to such company a subsidy in money and land along the line. Or, instead of paying cash, it may give bonds to the company, guaranteeing a certain rate of interest on the bonds, which then become marketable; while from the sale of lands along the line the company also derives a revenue.

The method adopted in Newfoundland, at first, was to pay an annual subsidy to a company who contracted to build the line, and to give them also grants of land along the line to the extent of five thousand acres of land for each mile of railway built, the land grants to be in alternate blocks of one mile along the line by eight miles in depth. The alternate sections were to be Government reserves, so as to prevent a monopoly of the land by a company.

Unfortunately, the first company with whom a contract was made became bankrupt after the building of only eighty-three miles, as far as Harbour Grace. This arrested railway development for a time. Had the work been undertaken by a financially strong company, the line, three hundred and forty miles in length, would have been completed in 1885. After this collapse twenty-seven miles of railway were

completed in 1888, connecting Placentia with the
Harbour Grace line. This was done under the Government of Sir Robert Thorburn. In 1889 Sir William
Whiteway again became Premier; and, nothing
daunted by the previous failure, he at once took steps
for the continuance and completion of his railway
policy.

In this instance he was fortunate enough to meet
with a contractor of high reputation and large experience, who was also possessed of ample means. This
was Robert G. Reid, Esq., the Thomas Brassey of
Canada, whose career as a contractor had placed him
in the front rank of constructors of public works, and
whose character gave sufficient assurance that whatever
he undertook would be skilfully and honestly executed.
The final contract for building a line *via* the Exploits
and Humber Valleys, and thence by Bay St. George
to Port-au-Basques, was signed on May 16, 1893; also
another contract, in which Mr. Reid undertook to
operate the new line, as well as the Placentia line, for
ten years from September, 1893. The terms of the
contracts were certainly favourable to the Colony.
For constructing and equipping payment was to be at
the rate of fifteen thousand six hundred dollars per mile,
in debentures of the Government of Newfoundland
bearing interest at three and a half per cent. per
annum. Under the operating contract, there was
to be a grant in fee-simple to the contractor of five
thousand acres of land for each one mile of main line
or branch railway throughout the entire lines of railway
to be operated. Should the line, therefore, be five

hundred miles in length, the land grant would be two millions five hundred thousand acres.

One noteworthy feature of the latter contract is that the line is to be operated for the first ten years at the expense of the contractor—this being the time when the returns would be lowest and the maintenance of the way most costly. Ere the ten years had expired, it might reasonably be expected that the revenue of the line would considerably exceed the working expenses. Further, the land grants, which, of course, are in a wilderness condition, can only be turned to profitable account by the contractor, by promoting settlement and the utilization of whatever land or minerals they may contain, thus securing an increase of the population and wealth of the country, and swelling the revenue. It is the interest of the contractor to turn these lands to the best account, and in doing so he will give increased employment to the people. The Government reserve of alternate sections will also be increased in value. Every way, therefore, the contract is favourable to the Colony. Without the railway and the contingent improvements which it brings, these lands must have remained for ever valueless.

It should also be carefully noted that Mr. Reid has accepted these land grants along the line instead of an annual subsidy in money, as payment for operating the line for the first ten years. The cost of such operation per annum is estimated at one hundred thousand dollars, so that in ten years the contractor will have spent about a million dollars. The revenue, during those first years, from passenger and goods traffic, must necessarily be small; so that for those lands the Colony escapes the heavy cost of working the line at first, and will assume management when the line becomes profitable. Moreover, Mr. Reid engaged to make grants of land along the line at thirty cents per acre—the Government upset price—to all *bonâ fide* settlers.

So vigorously has Mr. Reid prosecuted the work that only thirty miles remain, and the whole line will be completed to Port-au-Basques this year. By August a new steamer of the first class will be placed on the route between Port-au-Basques and Sydney, Cape Breton, now called Cabot Strait. This vessel will be fitted up with all modern improvements and arrangements for comfort, and will make the passage to Sydney in less than six hours. There, connection with the American railway system will be made, and passengers can thus reach all parts of the continent by rail. Mails will be conveyed by this route, and instead of a fortnightly mail, the people will enjoy the luxury of a tri-weekly mail. Business men will reap the benefit. A most attractive route for tourists and travellers will be established. Sportsmen of all classes will resort to the new land for deer-stalking, salmon and trout fishing; while those in search of fine scenery—sketching and photographing—will find, along the west coast and amid the lakes and valleys of the interior, all that they could desire. There is little doubt when hotel accommodation is provided that Newfoundland will become a favourite health-resort. Its cool, health-giving summer breezes will be enjoyed by those who can escape from the scorching heats of the great cities of Canada and the

United States. Before the great innovator, the railway, old things will pass away and a new and better social and industrial life will begin.

About the construction of the railway there can be but one opinion. The most competent judges pronounce it one of the best roads ever laid down in a new country. There is no flimsy work on it; all is solid and calculated to last. The road-bed is unsurpassed; the rails heavy and of the best material; the sleepers excellent; and the bridges and culverts, of granite and steel, are of the best construction. The passenger cars are of the same style as those used on the Canadian-Pacific Railway. Pullman cars are to form part of the equipment. In short, Mr. Reid has left nothing undone to make the line attractive and successful. The most liberal arrangements will be made for the promotion of a large passenger and goods traffic.

Is this railway likely to prove remunerative? Few lines, in a new country, present more abundant elements of success. In the valleys of Codroy, St. George's Bay, Bay of Islands, the Humber, Exploits, and Gander, which are either traversed or crossed by the railway, there are immense stretches of good land well adapted for settlement. Where the land is not arable it is in many places admirably adapted for cattle-raising, especially in the Exploits Valley, where there is an abundant supply of nutritious wild grasses in summer. Its proximity to English markets—only six or seven days' steaming—its excellent harbour, and its facilities for growing hay and root crops, all mark it out as a ranching district of great promise. An extensive lumbering business has already sprung up along these valleys. At Bay of Islands is one of the finest herring-fisheries in the world, which, aided by the means of transportation furnished by the railway, will be greatly enlarged. Extensive marble beds are also found here. A coal-field of great promise is crossed by the railway near Grand Lake, and iron is also reported to be found in its neighbourhood. The finest coal-field of the island is in St. George's Bay. Asbestos and other minerals are discovered at various points, and as the country is opened up and settled these mineral discoveries may be expected to increase. Fine harbours are available on both the western and eastern shores. In fact, the railway opens up the most valuable lands in the country. All these advantages combined give ample assurance of future prosperity for the railway. That a small Colony, by no means wealthy, has discovered such spirit, energy, and sagacity as to construct such a line, and to make provision for payment of interest on its cost, is certainly greatly to its credit; and it is now quite certain that it can shoulder the burden of debt incurred by its construction without any undue strain.

Those who desire fuller information regarding the new line of railway and the character of the country through which it passes, are referred to the author's "Handbook and Tourists' Guide" for Newfoundland. London: Trübner & Co.

CHAPTER VI.

Development of Mining in Newfoundland—First Copper Mine; how discovered—Predictions of Science—Value of Copper Export—Increasing demand for Copper—Iron Pyrites—Pilley's Island—Belle Isle Iron Mine; enormous deposit — Asbestos Mining — Discovery of Gold-bearing Quartz—Lead and Silver Ores—Petroleum on the West Coast.

FORTY years have elapsed since the first prospecting work was done in Newfoundland. People were slow to believe in the possibility of these grim old rocks containing mineral treasures of any value. One day, in the summer of 1857, a prospector named Smith McKay, when engaged in searching for minerals, dropped into the cottage of a fisherman in Tilt Cove, a fishing village in Notre Dame Bay, on the north-east coast. His quick eye caught sight of a piece of yellow-coloured stone that stood on the mantelshelf. On inquiry as to whence the curious stone came, he was told that one of the children had picked it up at the bottom of a cliff close at hand, and that it had fallen from a yellow rock in the face of the cliff. Of course, the poor fisherman had no idea that it was of any value, but McKay knew that he had found a deposit of rich copper ore. Ere many days had passed, a mining licence was secured, and in two or three years the quiet village was a scene of mining activity. In fifteen years this mine had produced 50,000 tons of copper ore, valued at $1,572,154, and nickel ore worth $32,740. It is still worked and shows no signs of exhaustion, and gives employment to some five hundred miners.

A few years after, Tilt Cove was completely eclipsed by the discovery of a still larger deposit of copper ore at Bett's Cove, a dozen miles farther south, from which, in four years, 125,556 tons of copper ore, valued at three millions of dollars, were exported. Three years later a new mine, which threw the other two into the shade, was opened at Little Bay, and for some years averaged an export of 20,000 tons per annum.

Other mines were opened in the same district and worked with more or less success. At the close of 1892, Mr. J. P. Howley, head of the Geological Survey, was able to report that the value of copper ore, regulus and ingots, exported from 1864 to the end of 1891 was $9,193,790.

Adding to this the value of iron pyrites exported from Pilley's Island up to the close of 1893—namely, $759,451—and of other minerals, such as lead, nickel, etc., together with copper ore, the aggregate reached $10,777,086, as the value of all the minerals exported from 1864 to the close of 1893. This was the outcome of that discovery of a bit of yellow rock on the mantel of a fisherman's cottage.

Mining has thus developed into one of the leading industries of the country, and, as we shall see presently, continues to expand as the island is explored and opened up. The staple mineral hitherto has been copper, and among the copper-producing countries of the world Newfoundland now ranks sixth. The demand

PLACENTIA RAILWAY STATION.

for this mineral is likely to increase in the future and its value to advance, owing to the rapid development of electricity as a motor power, copper being essential in its various practical applications. Copper-mining in the future is therefore likely to reach large dimensions in Newfoundland. The extent of country over which it has been found, and in which it may be looked for with a prospect of success, according to the verdict of science, is not less than five thousand square miles, so great is the development of the serpentine formation with which the copper ore is always associated. Only a mere fragment of these serpentines have yet been examined, and this mainly along the shores. What the interior will disclose, now that it is becoming opened out and settled, only time will tell.

NOTE.—Two names should be held in grateful remembrance in connection with the development of our mining industries. One is Charles F. Bennett, Esq., merchant, who was really the pioneer in mining. He was the first who reached the conclusion that the island contained minerals. He led the way in prospecting, and spent large sums of money in explorations for minerals. The discoverer of the first copper mine, Mr. Smith McKay, was a partner with Mr. Bennett. He held to his belief tenaciously, in spite of scoffs and ridicule, and confounded his opponents by working the first copper mine at Tilt Cove. The other name is Mr. Alexander Murray, F.G.S., who was for twenty years associated with Sir William Logan in the Geological Survey of Canada; and in 1864 took charge of the Newfoundland Geological Survey, and conducted it for twenty years, till the time of his death. His reports during those years were invaluable, as they made known the natural resources of the country and ultimately led to their development. He formed a high opinion of the island after exploring it for twenty years, and gave the sanction of his name, as a scientific man of high attainments, to the favourable reports of its natural capabilities.

Mr. McKay, who found the first copper deposit, did not visit that region by mere accident, or in a haphazard way. It was a suggestion from Sir William Dawson, the eminent geologist of Canada, that induced McKay to undertake a prospecting tour in that direction. From his knowledge of the geological structure of that part of the island, Sir W. Dawson was able to predict that copper and other ores would be found, just as Murchison predicted the discovery of gold in Australia. He was aware of the large development of the serpentines here—a fact of primary importance. They belong to what, in Canadian geology, is termed the Quebec group of the Lower Silurian series, and to the Middle or Lauzon division of that series—the metalliferous zone of North America. It is rich in copper ores, and is accompanied with silver, gold, nickel, and chromium ores. Now the Lauzon division is the one which is developed in North-Eastern Newfoundland. Knowing this, Dawson gave the hint to McKay to search this region, and hence his appearance at Tilt Cove. It is one of the triumphs of science which has never been before published, so far as the writer is aware. Had the predictive communication not been made, these mines in such an obscure region might have remained undiscovered to this day. Truly "knowledge is power."

It is to be noted that it is not in the serpentines that the copper ore is found, but in a chloritic slate, very ferruginous, which occurs both above and below the serpentine. Where the serpentines appear there is always a possibility that this ore-bearing chloritic slate may be found, so that the serpentines become a guide to prospectors. Where no serpentines are it is vain to look for ore; but there may be large developments of serpentine without any indications of ore. In the serpentine all the existing mines are situated. This mineral belt is about forty miles in length along the shore; its breadth inland is yet undetermined. There is good reason for believing that it extends right through the island to Bonne Bay and Bay of Islands on the western coast. Chromic iron has been found associated with these serpentines. They also frequently afford a beautiful variety of marble, as well as soapstone, asbestos, and talc. An eminent American mining expert, who examined this region some years ago, said, "The copper is a beautiful yellow sulphuret, and contains from eight to twelve per cent. of pure copper. I have never seen finer copper in the course of my experience. The character of the rocks in which it occurs is such as to give an assurance of perpetuity in the working. A more promising mining field for copper I have not seen. Newfoundland is destined to become one of the greatest copper-mining countries of the world."

Iron pyrites is another mineral abundant in the island. The only deposit yet worked on a large scale is at Pilley's Island, Exploits Bay. This splendid mine has been worked for several years. The ore is exported to the United States, and is used for the manufacture of sulphuric acid. The residuum of iron is used in the manufacture of the best steel. The ore gives fifty-four per cent. of sulphur, being superior to that of Spain. In 1894 the quantity shipped was thirty-eight thousand two hundred and fourteen tons, valued at one hundred and ninety-five thousand seven hundred and eighty dollars. Adjoining it is another deposit, said to be much larger. It awaits capital for its development. The whole export of iron pyrites in 1893 was fifty-eight thousand three hundred and eleven tons, the value of which was two hundred and sixty-four thousand three hundred and eighty-four dollars.

It was not till very recently that iron ore in workable quantities was found in the island. As in the case of copper, its discovery was somewhat romantic. In Conception Bay, about twelve miles distant from St. John's, lies Belle Isle, six miles in length and three in breadth. It was long noted for its excellent soil and the value of its farm products. No one dreamed that it held any minerals. Under the vegetable soil, however, there were extensive strata of rock of a dusky red colour, which cropped out at several places in the cliffs around the shores of the island. Blocks of this reddish rock were detached by the weather and lay on the beach, but no one took any notice of these boulders. A fisherman, who was going to St. John's, chanced to observe that these rocks were much heavier than ordinary blocks, and it occurred to him that they would make good ballast. He piled a number of them into his little craft, and when leaving St. John's on his return trip, having obtained a cargo of goods, he left his ballast on one of the wharves. Some one with a sharper eye than his fellows was struck with the appearance and weight of the stones, and suspected that they were metalliferous. He sent a sample to England for analysis, and was speedily informed that it was a rich iron ore. An exploration on the island followed, and the red rock was traced under the soil for a considerable distance. Soon the area was covered with mining licences; and when the strata were partially uncovered, one of the finest deposits of iron ore in the world was found. An expert estimated that two of the bands included in the leases contain forty million tons of ore, so that practically it is inexhaustible.

This discovery took place a little over two years ago, and already a costly mining plant has been erected, and arrangements made for shipping the ore. The first shipments were made towards the close of last year, and this year operations are likely to be conducted on a large scale. The "Nova Scotia Steel Company," of New Glasgow, are the lessees of the property, which consists of four grants, each being one square mile. The ore is brown hematite, and contains from forty-eight to fifty-six per cent. of metallic iron. At present it is used by the lessees for intermixture with Nova Scotia ores, the resultant pig-iron producing a superior class of steel. It is likely to find a market in the United States for a similar purpose.

One remarkable feature of this mine, in which it differs from most iron mines, is the extraordinary ease with which the ore can be extracted. It lies near the surface, having only a thin soil above it which is readily removed, laying bare the deposit for acres in extent. It has a jointed cleavage, causing it to break out in rhomboidal masses of all sizes. Blasting, except to a very small extent, is therefore unnecessary. A few men with crowbars and pickaxes can raise many tons a day. It would be difficult to find elsewhere a mine that can be worked at such a small cost. All things considered, the value of such a mine must be immense.

It does not, however, by any means include all the iron ore in Belle Isle. The remainder of the island is under licences of search by various parties, and developments are likely to be made this year. There is a strong probability that smelting works will be erected on the spot, especially as coal has been found along the new line of railway.

This, however, is not the whole story of this iron deposit. It crops out for miles along the opposite northern shore of Conception Bay, as far as Island Cove. The prospector has been at work here; numerous mining licences have been taken out, and samples of the ore, which is reported to be very extensive, have yielded, on analysis, sixty-two per cent. of metallic iron. A wealthy mining firm in England has been negotiating with the licensees, and has purchased the property, subject to an examination by their own expert, who is now on his way here.

It has also been long known that in Western Newfoundland magnetic iron ore has been discovered at many points; and at Port-au-Port, near Bay St. George, a very valuable deposit of chromic iron has been found.

NEW IRON-MINE, BELLE ISLE: APPARATUS FOR SHIPPING ORE.

This mine has been leased by an American Company, who are about to work it on an extensive scale. It would thus appear that Newfoundland is, rapidly becoming an iron-producing, as well as a copper-producing country. "Facts are stubborn things," and cannot be set aside. It is also clear that the attention of mining capitalists has been drawn to consider its capabilities, and that its prospects as a field for investments in mining enterprises are widening rapidly.

The next most important mineral found in the island is asbestos, but the mining of this valuable article is yet in its infancy. Scientific men, years ago, predicted that asbestos would be found in the island. Their opinion was based on the fact that the metamorphic rocks and serpentines of the eastern townships of Quebec and the Gaspe Peninsula, in which the Canadian asbestos is found, dip under the Gulf of St. Lawrence, appear again on the west coast of Newfoundland, extend many miles inland, and probably entirely across the island. "The serpentines," says a high authority, "with the granulite dykes which everywhere intersect them, contain vast deposits of minerals, and are to-day nearly virgin fields, except in the immediate coast-line, for the prospector or miner, and certain to become, in the immediate future, the seat of great mining operations."

During the last three years search has been made for asbestos, and the predictions of the geologists have been verified to a very considerable extent. The "Halifax Asbestos Company," the "Newfoundland Mineral Syndicate"—an English Mining Company—and a

H

number of individual adventurers, have been engaged in the search for asbestos, and their labours, so far, show very satisfactory results, and prove the field to be a large and valuable one. The neighbourhood of Port-au-Port has attracted most attention, but now that the railway has penetrated this region, a great impetus will be given to asbestos-mining, which ere long may become an important branch of mining industry.

It is a fact of primary importance that this island, so productive in copper and iron ores, is also proved to contain extensive coal-fields. Since the visit of Professor J. B. Jukes to Newfoundland, in 1842, the existence of a coal area of considerable extent, in the region around Bay St. George, has been known. This distinguished geologist, when a young man, spent a year in the examination of the island. He gave special attention to the carboniferous region on the west coast. In the south side of Bay St. George, near Crabb's River, he discovered a fine seam of excellent cannel coal between three and four feet in thickness. After a careful examination of the region, he calculated that this coal-field was about twenty-five miles wide by ten in length, and in all probability would be found a productive coal area. Mr. J. P. Howley, F.G.S., now at the head of the Geological Survey, discovered another coal-seam in this region, on Robinson's Brook, about nine miles from its mouth, its thickness being four feet. Two other seams occur in the same section, the three seams giving a thickness of eight feet of coal. In 1889 a more thorough examination of this coal district was carried out, resulting in the discovery that the whole of the coal seams in Bay St. George's Trough aggregate about twenty-seven feet in thickness. "To illustrate the importance," says Mr. Howley in his report, "of what such information would mean, it may be stated that an aggregate of twenty-seven feet of coal, provided the seams maintained their ascertained thickness throughout, should for every square mile of superficial area they may be found to underlie, contain about 25,920,000 tons of coal."

There is another trough known as "the inland trough of Humber River and Grand Lake," which will probably be found not less valuable than that of Bay St. George, and its importance is enhanced by the fact that the railway passes through it, so that its development will speedily follow. Here Mr. Howley has made some most important discoveries lately. He has established beyond all doubt that the coal-measures here form a continuous trough from about a mile to the west of Aldery Brook, to a point on the railway-line, *a total distance in a straight line of eleven miles.* Towards its eastern end the trough widens considerably. "Eighteen outcrops of coal were uncovered here, representing nine separate seams. The coal throughout is of good quality, some of it excellent." From one of these seams a car-load of coal was taken over the line to St. John's where it was tested with most satisfactory results. The analysis of it in England proved that the quality was excellent. One of the seams, marked No. 6 on Mr. Howley's plan, "is made up of two layers of excellent bright black coal divided by a layer of carbonaceous shale. The lower coal is three feet six inches thick, and the upper, two feet eight inches, making in all six feet two inches of good coal." Of course much remains to be done before its full extent and value can be determined; but that it is a most promising coal-field is put beyond reasonable doubt. If present indications prove to be reliable, here is a coal area from which the whole island could be supplied with coal, including household consumption, smelting of ores, and supplies for railway purposes. The region is but forty miles from Bay of Islands, where there is an excellent shipping port.

In September of last year the people were startled by the announcement that a gold-bearing quartz reef had been discovered at Cape Broyle, about forty miles south of St. John's. Here an experienced gold prospector had been at work for some time; and after sinking a shaft on a quartz vein, he took out samples which were forwarded for assay to the eminent firm of Johnson, Matthey & Co., London. Their assay showed that the quartz contained nearly three ounces of gold and one ounce and eleven pennyweights of silver to the ton of two thousand two hundred and forty pounds of quartz, value sixty dollars. This was not all. Samples of the grey rock of the country underlying the quartz were also sent, and yielded eight pennyweights twelve grains of gold. There was no trickery or deception in the matter, the transaction was *bonâ fide*. It was also stated that the samples sent for assay were not picked specimens, but taken at random from the heap. A gold fever speedily broke out, and in a short time thirty square miles around the quartz vein first opened were covered by licences of search, to which more have been added since.

It would be rash to build any large speculations on this discovery until the whole has been tested by further operations. All is yet *in gremio Jovis*. But it is a fact of no little importance that a quartz reef, yielding three ounces of gold to the ton, has been discovered in Newfoundland. Add to this that previously gold had been found at many places, but only in small quantities, such as would not pay for the working. Further, eminent geologists—such as the late Mr. Murray, the first director of the Geological Survey—had long ago predicted the discovery of gold from the character of the formations in many districts, where the rocks, he pronounced, were the equivalents of the gold-bearing formations of Nova Scotia. Other scientific men declared that gold might be looked for with a strong probability of success.

Should the island, in addition to the minerals previously named, also yield gold in paying quantities, it is needless to say that this would create a new era in its history. A gold-mining company has been formed to carry on operations at Cape Broyle as soon as spring opens. Numerous individuals and small syndicates are also preparing for active operations. There is said to be a very large development of quartz veins at Cape Broyle, and time will tell whether they are auriferous. At present it can only be said that matters look very hopeful.

The first discovery of lead ore was made many years ago at La Manche, near the north-eastern extremity of

Placentia Bay. The workings here were carried on for several years, in a vein from three to six feet wide; but skill and capital were wanting, and the enterprise collapsed. The shores of Placentia Bay are highly metalliferous, and a silver mine has lately been opened here, known as "Silver Cliff Mine," which presents very promising appearances. It has been taken up by foreign capitalists, who will carry on active operations this summer. It is believed to be of great value, and has brought a high price.

In 1875 a rich deposit of lead ore was found at Port-au-Port, and was worked for a time with very promising results; but as this locality is on the so-called "French shore," the Imperial authorities ordered the works to be discontinued, the French having entered a protest against mining here as *an interference with their fishery rights*. We had thus a practical illustration that Newfoundland is not mistress in her own territory.

In addition to metallic ores, the island yields many substances of economic value which will be turned to profitable account as the country becomes settled. Gypsum of the best quality is distributed more profusely and in greater volume in the carboniferous districts than in any part of the American continent of the same extent. In Bay St. George and Codroy the developments of gypsum are immense. Marbles, too, of almost every shade of colour have been found in various places, on both the western and eastern shores, especially at Bay of Islands. Granite of the finest quality, building stones, whetstones, limestones, roofing slate are in ample profusion.

These materials will require time for their development; but recently the discovery of petroleum has been made, and this can be turned to immediate account. On the western coast, north of Cow Head, there is an extensive tract of country in which it was reported long since that oil had been seen floating on the surface of lakes and marshes. Fifty years ago, Mr. Reeks, an English naturalist, visited this part of the island for the purpose of studying the animals and vegetables of the region. He was the first to notice this oil, and in his articles which appeared in the *Zoologist* he made special mention of it. So impressed was he with the appearance of one locality that he endeavoured to form a company to work it, but was not successful. Within the last three years explorations have been made and two companies formed. Borings have been going on for some months under well-qualified engineers, and at length with successful results. The company named "The Canadian Petroleum Company," operating near St. Paul's Inlet, have "struck oil" at a depth of a thousand feet. The quantity is reported to be very large, and the quality, on analysis, is found to be excellent. The second company are reported to have been equally successful.

It is said that the oil shows itself over a large area. Mr. R. G. Reid, contractor for the railway, holds considerable land concessions in the petroleum district. The facilities for shipping the oil are said to be excellent. Here, then, is another promising field for industrial enterprise.

CHAPTER VII.

Newfoundland as an Agricultural and Lumbering Country—Extent of Arable and Grazing Land—Value of Farm Products and Domestic Animals—Liberality of Land Acts—Homestead Act—Paper Pulp Act—Forest Wealth—The Climate.

In the chapter on railway extension some general idea was furnished of the agricultural lands of the island which are now rendered accessible by the transinsular line of railway. These are of very considerable extent and value, and are capable of sustaining a large population; while the forest wealth is also very great, and can now be turned to profitable account.

To many it will still be a matter of surprise to find Newfoundland spoken of as an agricultural country. The old idea that it is a dismal fog-enveloped island, whose savage climate and poor soil preclude all attempts at agriculture, is still widely prevalent. No doubt it is true that there are wide tracts in the island irreclaimably barren; others unfit for arable purposes, though excellent for grazing; and others covered with marshes and what the people call "barrens." Lakes, rivers, and ponds occupy perhaps a third or a fourth of the surface of the whole island. But the same holds good of much of the United States and Canada, where vast areas are hopelessly barren and could never repay cultivation.

The agricultural lands of the island lie in belts, mainly along the valleys through which the principal rivers run, or around the heads of the great bays and the margins of the smaller streams.

If we take the whole area of the island to be forty-two thousand square miles, and deduct from this as much as one-third for lakes, rivers, and ponds, we have twenty-eight thousand square miles, of which fully a fourth, or seven thousand square miles, or four millions four hundred and eighty thousand acres, are available for settlement, either as arable land or for grazing purposes. Such an extent of land is capable, in itself, of sustaining a very large population in comfort. But when we add to the agricultural the forest and mineral resources, and the innumerable other industrial employments that spring up along with mining, farming, and lumbering, it is surely no exaggeration to say that millions might, and one day will, find comfortable homes in this great island, in which the inhabitants, at present, do not exceed two hundred and ten thousand. These are not the random assertions of enthusiastic optimists; they are warranted by solid facts which cannot be set aside. The evidence in support of these conclusions is drawn from the reports of the Geological Survey, which has been going on for thirty years, and is conducted by scientific men who are thoroughly trustworthy; also from the reports of the Government surveyors, who have been for years engaged in mapping the Crown lands; as well as from the accounts given by residents, by intelligent travellers, and others who have visited the various sections of the island.

Perhaps a still more convincing proof of the agricultural capabilities of Newfoundland may be drawn from what has already been accomplished in the cultivation of the soil and the rearing of farm-stock. Owing to the causes already enumerated—the long-continued prohibition of settlement; the want of roads and railways till a comparatively recent date, so that the larger tracts of good land were inaccessible; and to the almost exclusive employment of the people in fishing—the progress of agriculture has been very slow. The last census—that of 1891—shows that only 179,215 acres of land are yet occupied; and that the value of the growing crops that year was $1,562,398. Further, the income derived from cattle and other domestic animals that year was $732,000; making the value of the total agricultural products of the island to be $2,295,398 in 1891. The same census gave the value of the live stock—horses, cattle, sheep, etc.—at $1,189,413.

These are surely creditable results of the very limited industry yet devoted to farming. It should also be remembered that the cultivation of the land is as yet confined to the neighbourhood of the settlements and towns, and the portions opened by the roads which connect them. There are but few farms more than three or four miles from the sea-coast; so that only the poorest portions of the soil have yet been brought under culture, and in the regions least favoured in regard to climate—the eastern shore.

The law which regulates the sale or letting of Crown lands for agricultural, lumbering, or mining purposes is of the most liberal character, and well calculated to promote the settlement of the country. Land can be purchased direct from the Government at the upset price of thirty cents per acre, upon the condition that the grantee shall, within five years from the date of the grant, *bonâ fide* clear and cultivate ten acres for every hundred acres comprised in the grant. Also, licences of occupation of unappropriated Crown lands are issued on payment of a fee of five dollars for each one hundred and sixty acres, and for not more than six thousand four hundred acres, subject to the condition that the licensee shall, within two years, settle upon the land one family for each one hundred and sixty acres, and for a period of five years cause to be cleared at least two acres per year for every one hundred acres so licensed, and continue the same under cultivation for a period of ten years from the expiration of the said five years; he shall then be entitled to a grant in fee of the said land. For those who are disposed to speculate in land, and to promote emigration by the settlement of families in the neighbourhood of each other, and within a short distance of the railway, such an arrangement is most advantageous. Mr. Reid, the contractor, will sell the land he owns along the line to settlers, on the same terms as the Government—thirty cents per acre.

The Homestead Law—one of the most beneficial ever enacted for the farming population—is in operation here. By it any person settling in wilderness lands, to cultivate and improve the same, and erect a dwelling-house thereon, shall be entitled to an estate of homestead not exceeding twenty acres, and such homestead shall be exempt from attachment, levy, or execution sale for the payment of debts or other purposes, etc.

There is also a law called "The Paper Pulp Act," of an exceedingly liberal character, under which licences are granted to cut timber for the purpose of manufacturing paper or paper pulp. Several companies have taken up lands under this Act, and are now erecting machinery for the manufacture of paper pulp. The materials for such an industry are almost inexhaustible, while the demand for it is extending rapidly.

The forest wealth of the Colony still unutilized is immense. These forests are chiefly along the banks of the larger rivers and their tributaries, and around the heads of the bays. The principal varieties of the indigenous forest growths are white pine, white and black spruce, tamarack or larch, fir, yellow and white birch. The yellow birch, which abounds around Bay St. George, is said to be equal in durability to the English oak, and, with the spruces and larches, is admirably adapted for ship-building purposes. The lumber trade, already developed along the portion of the new line of railway which has been completed and operated, furnishes ample proof of the forest resources of the country, and gives good promise for the future. The pine shipped to England commands the best prices in the markets.

Erroneous ideas regarding the climate of Newfoundland have been quite as prevalent as the delusions in reference to its soil. Popularly it is supposed to be enveloped in fogs during a good part of the year. These fogs are engendered on the Great Banks by the meeting of the Arctic Current and the Gulf Stream. When southerly or south-easterly winds blow, this fog is rolled in on the southern and south-eastern shores of the island, covering the bays, creeks, and headlands with a thick curtain of vapour. The fog seldom penetrates far inland. When the coasts are shrouded in vapour the sun is often shining brightly a few miles from the shore, and the atmosphere is dry and balmy. The fogs are thus but partial in their influence, being confined to the southern and south-eastern shores of the island. On the western shore, after Cape Ray is passed, fogs are almost unknown. The same holds good of the northern and north-eastern shores as far south as Bonavista. The great interior is free from fogs. Besides, it is only during a portion of the year, and when certain winds blow, that the fogs engendered on the Banks are wafted shoreward. During three-fourths of the year the westerly winds carry the vapours across the Atlantic, and the British Isles get the benefit of their moisture. However unpleasant and gloomy these fogs may be, it must be remembered they are not prejudicial to health.

Taken as a whole, the climate of the island is more temperate and more favourable to health than that of the neighbouring continent. The fierce summer heats of Canada and the United States, and the intense cold of their winters, are unknown here. It is but rarely, and then only for a few hours, that the thermometer sinks below zero in winter, while the summer range rarely exceeds eighty degrees, and generally does not rise above seventy. Like all insular climates, that of Newfoundland is subject to sudden changes, and its salubrity is evidenced by the robust, healthy appearance of the people. Their clothing in winter does not require to be much warmer than that worn in Britain at the same season of the year. Open fireplaces are sufficient to warm the houses, and free exercise in the open air is attainable at all seasons.

Thus, in the American sense of the term, Newfoundland is by no means a cold country; but it partakes of the general character of the North American climate, and is, therefore, much colder than a country in the same latitude of the Old World. Its latitude corresponds to that of France, but its climate is very different. Winter sets in, as a rule, in the beginning of December, and lasts till the end of March or middle of April. Snow-storms then are not uncommon, and when the icy particles are hurled on the wings of a fierce north-easter it is safest to keep within doors. Winter, however, is the season of social enjoyments of all kinds, and is far from being unpleasant. Nothing can be more exhilarating than the bracing air of a fine winter's day, with the hard crisp snow underfoot and a bright sun overhead. In fact, winter is the most enjoyable time of the year. Vegetation is very rapid once it sets in. The summers are delightful.

There is nothing in the climate to interfere with agriculture. The destructive tornadoes that often spread havoc in certain portions of the North American continent are unknown. Even thunder-storms are very rare, and seldom if ever prove injurious.

CHAPTER VIII.

THE FISHERIES.

Fisheries the Staple Industry of the People—Their Value—Arctic Current essential to Fish-life—Food of the Cod—Annual Catch of Cod—Fisheries Department—Stability of the Fisheries—Seal Fishery—Its Value—Mode of pursuing it—Herring Fishery—Salmon and Lobster Fisheries—Improvements needed.

IT was said of Amsterdam that "its foundations were laid on herring-bones"—the herring fishery having given the first impetus to its prosperity. With equal truth it might be said of the Colony of Newfoundland, that its prosperity rests upon a foundation of codfish-bones. The cod and other fisheries have long been, and must long continue to be, the main industries by which its people earn their daily bread. On the export of its fishery products the trade of the country mainly depends. Other industries are developing, especially in recent years; but in importance they do not as yet compare with the great fishing interests. The products of the fisheries constitute nearly four-fifths of the entire exports of the Colony. Out of a population of 210,000 there are about 56,000 engaged in catching and curing fish, and 12,000 in all other occupations. The mean annual value of the fishery exports, in recent years, has been about $6,600,000. To this must be added the

FISH-MAKING IN THE NARROWS OF ST. JOHN'S.

value of the fish consumed by the people in the country, estimated at $400,000; so that the average annual value of the whole fisheries of the country is about $7,000,000. The total value of the Canadian fisheries, including the salt-water, lake, and river fisheries, is about $19,000,000. The annual value of the Norwegian fisheries is about the same as that of Newfoundland.— $7,000,000; that of the United States about $14,000,000. The value of the whole British American fisheries (including Newfoundland) is now over $25,000,000. British European sea fisheries are estimated at $36,000,000.

Cold-water seas are essential to the life of the commercial food-fishes. In the tropical seas, or even in the warm waters of the Gulf Stream, they could not exist, any more than the Arctic hare could thrive in the Torrid zone. The Arctic current, which washes the coasts of Labrador, Newfoundland, Canada, and part of the United States, chilling the atmosphere, and bearing on its bosom huge ice-argosies, is the source of the vast fish-wealth which has been drawn on for ages, and which promises to continue for ages to come. Wanting this cold river in the ocean, the cod, seals, herrings, mackerel, halibut, hake, etc., which now crowd the northern seas, would be entirely absent.

It is not, however, owing to its temperature alone that the Labrador current is favourable to the development of the commercial fishes, though that is essential to their growth. The cold current brings with it the food on which these fishes thrive, and the supply is one that can never fail. So far from being unfavourable to the production of life, the Arctic seas and the great rivers which they send forth are swarming with minute forms of life, constituting, in the words of Professor Hind, "in many places a living mass, a vast ocean of living slime; and the all-pervading life which exists there affords the true solution of the problem which has so often presented itself to those engaged in the great fisheries—where the food comes from which gives sustenance to the countless millions of fish which swarm on the coasts of Labrador, Newfoundland, the Dominion of Canada, and the United States, or wherever the Arctic current exerts an active influence." This living slime of the ocean is most abundant in the coldest water, and especially in the neighbourhood of ice. The ice-laden current from Baffin's Bay brings with it those forms of marine life, from the diatom to the minute crustacean, from the minute crustacean to the crab and prawn, together with the molluscous animals and starfish in vast profusion. The "slime-food" sustains the minute crustaceans; and these in their turn furnish food for the herring which swarm on the shores, in the bays, and especially on the Grand Banks. The herring, with multitudes of smaller forms, are devoured by the cod. When the cod is assimilated by man, the great circle of Nature is complete. As long, then, as the Arctic current flows, the existence of the cod fishery of Newfoundland is assured.

Very wonderful are these great processes of Nature. These vast ice-fields, and countless battalions of icebergs, the terror of mariners, sailing majestically past these shores, and often grounding along Labrador and in the bays of Newfoundland, bring with them slime-food for the microscopic crustaceans, which sustain the caplin, the squid, the herring, and many other marine creatures. Then comes the all-devouring cod, and finds a rich banquet spread for it. The mackerel, the hake, the haddock, the salmon, all find abundant supplies. In this way the great fishing interests, on which millions rely for their daily bread, are as dependent on the Arctic current as the farming interests on the rain and sunshine which ripen the crops. Here, too, is an illustration of Nature's great law of compensation. While the bleak shores of these northern regions are almost tenantless wildernesses, the encompassing seas are swarming with vast varieties of marine life, and the nobler forms of food-fishes.

The sea-harvest, for which no ploughing or sowing is needed, is that to which the people of Newfoundland at present mainly look for their sustenance. By far the most important of its fisheries is that of the cod. The products of this fishery constitute nearly three-fourths of the whole fishery exports of the Colony. It is the largest cod fishery in the world. The cod exports average 1,350,000 quintals of 112 lbs. weight. Norway comes nearest to Newfoundland, its export being an average of 750,000 quintals. The cod are taken on the shores of the island, on the Great Banks, a day's sail from the shore, and along the coast of Labrador. It is wonderful to think that almost from the days of Cabot, or during the last four hundred years, the cod fishery has been prosecuted; and notwithstanding the enormous drafts every year, there are no signs of exhaustion. There are to-day more fishermen than ever plying their avocations in these teeming waters. The Bank fishery is now chiefly prosecuted by the French from St. Pierre, and the Americans. Newfoundlanders had at one time almost abandoned the Bank fishery, occupying themselves mainly with the shore and Labrador fishery; but seven years ago there was a revival of the Bank fishery, and over 3,000 Newfoundland fishermen were engaged in it. There were 199 vessels, having a tonnage of 11,520 tons, employed in it in 1891; but there has been a decrease since that date. About a fifth of the whole cod export is taken on Labrador.

The annual aggregate catch of cod in North American waters, including the fisheries on the Banks by French, Americans, Canadians, and Newfoundlanders, is estimated at four millions of quintals, or about two hundred millions of codfish. Apparently this enormous annual catch makes little impression on the cod-kingdoms. In this fact, we have good ground for believing that this source of wealth to Newfoundland cannot fail in the future. Here is a sure and permanent harvest for the reaping; though it varies considerably year by year, being dependent on winds and weather.

Within the last seven years the Government and people have awoke to the necessity of regulating and protecting the fisheries. A Department of Fisheries has been created, with a commissioner at its head, and a skilful, scientific superintendent in charge of the practical work. The fisheries are now placed under well-considered rules and regulations, and it may be reasonably hoped that not only will any decline in the fisheries be arrested, but that localities in which exhaustion of the waters may have occurred by overfishing or from other causes, will be re-stocked by artificial propagation; while improvements in the methods of cure will also be carried out.

Looking to the future, there is every reason to hope that these fisheries, being wisely managed, will increasingly become a source of wealth to the country. The demand for cod is not likely to fall off. Catholic countries alone, in connection with the season of Lent and the weekly fast on Fridays, spend annually a million pounds sterling in the purchase of cod taken in North American waters. So far from declining in value, the price of Newfoundland cod has advanced from fifty to seventy-five per cent. within the last thirty years. This fishery, therefore, is a profitable industry that can never fail.

THE SEAL FISHERY.*

Next to the cod fishery the most valuable is that of the seal. While the cod fishery has been prosecuted for four hundred years, the seal fishery is not quite one hundred years old. The attention of the people was so absorbed in the pursuit of the cod in earlier years, that they neglected the oleaginous treasures which the great ice-fields floating south every year brought within their reach. It was not till the beginning of the present century that the seal-hunters began to force their way through the crystal ramparts by which Nature had so long protected these helpless innocents. Then the nursery of countless mother-seals was invaded and

* See pp. 173-188 for an illustrated account of the great seal-hunt.

transformed into a slaughter-house, red with the blood of their murdered darlings, slain in their icy cradles, and became a scene of horror and death. Such is the seal-hunt of to-day, involving each year a vast destruction of old and young seal life for the benefit of man.

On the floating fields of Arctic ice the seals bring forth their young about the end of February. In four or five weeks these "white-coats," as the young are called, are in the best condition for being taken, and their fat then yields the finest oil. The daring hunters dash into these ice-masses in their vessels, and when the seal-herd is struck they leap on the ice, kill the young seals in myriads by a blow on the nose; then, with their sharp knives, detach the skin with the adhering fat from the carcase, which is left on the ice, while the "pelts" are dragged over the ice to the ship, and carried to port, where the fat is manufactured into oil, and the skins are salted and exported.

In the earlier years of the seal fishery, stout schooners of 50 to 200 tons were employed. They were fitted to encounter the ice, and with the skill, hardihood, and daring of the captains and men, the industry was prosecuted with great success. In those days the seals were more numerous than at present, and were taken nearer the shore. The annual catch ranged from 300,000 to 500,000 seals. In 1831 the largest catch ever taken was put on record—686,836 seals. In 1840 the number brought in was 631,385. In 1857 some 400 vessels of 60 to 200 tons, their united crews numbering 13,000 men, took part in the fishery. After that came a decline for some years,

SEALING STEAMER LOADED, AND ENTERING ST. JOHN'S HARBOUR.

probably owing to storms and the unfavourable condition of the ice. In 1863 the great innovator steam entered the field, and the advantages of steamers were speedily felt. The sailing vessels were gradually superseded, till, in 1882, there were twenty-five large steamers, and but a few schooners. At present there are eighteen or nineteen steamers from 350 to 500 tons burthen engaged in the fishery. The largest load of seals ever brought in was by the steamer *Neptune*, Captain Blandford, whose cargo numbered nearly 42,000, value $103,750.

The average catch now ranges from 300,000 to 360,000. Depending as it does on the condition of the ice and the direction and force of the winds, this fishery is exceedingly uncertain, and sometimes ends in failure. Such has been the case this year (1897), when the catch does not exceed 135,000. In 1892 it was 390,000. In 1893, 174,900.

The value of seal oil has declined of late years owing to the use of crude petroleum and some kinds of vegetable oils in manufactures in which seal oil was once exclusively used. The price of skins, however, has advanced. Formerly the average annual value of the seal fishery was a million dollars.

The following figures show the value of the products of the seal fishery since 1885:—

DATE.	SEALS.
1885	238,596
1886	272,656
1887	230,355
1888	286,464
1889	335,627

Date.	Seals.
1890	220,846
1891	364,854
1892	390,174
1893	174,997
1894	159,826
1895	270,058
1896	187,517
1897 (estimated)	135,000

The value of the seal fishery is enhanced by the fact that it is prosecuted at a time when other northern countries are locked in icy fetters, and their people idle. But by the 10th of March each year the hardy Newfoundland seal-hunters embark, and amid the crashing floes they capture their prey in six or seven weeks. Thus the seal fishery interferes with no other industry, and the men who take part in it can follow up the summer fishery or engage in the cultivation of the soil.

The Herring Fishery.

The herring fishery has been sadly neglected. Had it been prosecuted with skill and energy—had care been bestowed on the cure and packing, and had it been placed, years ago, under proper regulations, it might to-day have approached the cod fishery in value. In the annual report of the Department of Fisheries for the present year, it is stated that the value of the export of herring does not now exceed $250,000, whereas it might be made to yield three millions of dollars annually. The quality of the herrings cannot be surpassed, and the quantity is enormous. The chief seats of the herring fishery are Fortune, Placentia, St. George's Bays, and Bay of Islands. On Labrador herring of the finest quality are taken. The Fisheries Board are using strenuous efforts to improve and extend this valuable fishery. Fifty-three American vessels visited Placentia Bay this year, and took away 50,000 barrels of frozen herring, paying only a dollar a barrel. Had these been cured and packed on the spot, they would have realized about seven or eight dollars in the foreign market; and the handling of the fish, the making of barrels, and the freighting of vessels, would have given employment to large numbers. All this is lost by the present method of selling them at a low price to the Americans in a frozen condition.

Salmon Fishery.

The export of salmon is comparatively small, not exceeding in value $100,000 per annum. It is either pickled or put in hermetically sealed tins. By neglect, the salmon rivers, naturally among the finest, have suffered sadly. Ignorance and greed of immediate gain led to "barring" the rivers with nets at the time when the salmon are ascending to spawn; while other destructive practices prevailed, so that in many of the finest streams the salmon are almost exterminated. The Fisheries Board have been for some time grappling with these evils, by placing wardens to prevent "barring," and to keep the streams from being polluted by sawdust. By proper protection these streams will be restored to their former productiveness and become one of the valuable resources of the country.

The Lobster Fishery.

The lobster fishery has expanded greatly during the last fifteen or twenty years. It now gives employment to 4000 persons, and is valued at $600,000 per annum. The Fisheries Board have been for six years carrying on the artificial propagation of lobsters at seventy different stations on the shores of the great bays, and with excellent results. The immense number of 450,000,000 of lobster ova are hatched artificially every year and planted in the waters. The fishery is also placed under strict regulations.

These fisheries, then, constitute another, and at present by far the most valuable of the resources of the country. These "silvery quarries of the sea" are inexhaustible. They are now worth $7,000,000; but it is not too much to say that their value might readily be increased to $12,000,000 annually, if science were brought to bear more completely on their management, and capital and enterprise were more fully directed to their development and improvement. Antiquated methods, that have retarded the advance of the fisheries, must be abandoned. The "supplying," or "truck system," has got its death-blow; but it is yet far from dead. It must be rooted out before any substantial progress can be made. The altered conditions of modern days must be more clearly realized by those whose capital is embarked in the fisheries; and they must gird themselves to meet the keen competition in foreign markets which has been recently developed, and which calls for all their vigilance and energies. The aid of science in connection with the fisheries must be more extensively invoked. Here it is where Government can do much by a judicious and liberal support of a well-organized Department of Fisheries, which should co-operate with those who direct fishing operations, and ship the products to foreign markets. A good beginning has been made in the Department of Fisheries, and fair progress secured. What is needed is more thorough sympathy and support for those who are trying to introduce improved methods and new ideas in the working and protection of the fisheries.

We have seen the security on which these great industries rest. The laws of Nature provide for their stability. While the bays and shores of the island abound with fish, the Great Banks, with their swarming fish-life, and their immense extent of 600 miles, are within a day's sail; while Labrador, with its coast-line of 1100 miles, and the finny treasures of its waters, is under the jurisdiction of Newfoundland. Nothing is wanting but skill, labour, and perseverance to make the Newfoundland fisheries one of the most prosperous industries in the world.

CHAPTER IX.

Form of Government—Evolution of Self-government—How the Colony is Governed—Vote by Ballot—Manhood Suffrage—Working of Responsible Government—Education called for as a Safeguard — Judicature — Constabulary — Fire Department — Post Office.

IN preceding chapters the evolution of popular government in Newfoundland has been described. It was worked out through a slow and difficult process and amid many hindrances. But in battling for their liberties, the people gained intelligence, vigour, courage ; and by activity, combined with self-control and patient endurance, they at length won their freedom. We have seen the vicissitudes and trials through which the Colony passed, and the flagrant misgovernment which so long retarded its prosperity. Happily, all this has been left behind. Self-government, in its most advanced form, has been reached—a "government for the people and by the people." No more striking contrast could be presented than the government of the rough Fishing Admirals, or even that of the migratory governors and the captains of the Royal Navy, and the government of to-day, when the Legislature is elected by universal suffrage, and its members are responsible to the people. Every man on reaching the age of twenty-one, unless he be a criminal or a pauper, is entitled to a vote in selecting representatives for his district in the local Parliament. Representative government, which was the initiatory step, was granted in 1832, and twenty-three years later was completed by the concession of "responsible government." This is nothing more than the application of the principles of the British Constitution to the government of the Colony. It provided that "the country should be governed according to the well-understood wishes of the people." The party who are sustained by a majority in the Legislature have at their disposal the appointments to the principal offices in the Colony. By them, too, the Executive Council is selected. The House of Assembly is elected by the people; the Legislative Council is appointed by the Queen.

This, then, is the form of government by which the affairs of the Colony are at present regulated. It consists of a Governor, who is appointed by the Crown, his salary being paid by the Colony; an Executive Council, selected from the party commanding a majority in the Legislature, and consisting of not more than seven members; a Legislative Council of not more than fifteen members, nominated by the Governor in Council, and holding office for life; and a House of Assembly, at present consisting of thirty-six members, elected every four years by the votes of the people. In the governing body, thus consisting of the Governor representing the Queen, the Legislative Council representing the House of Lords, and the House of Assembly, is vested collectively the legislative power. They have also exclusive jurisdiction over such matters as the public debt and the public property; raising money on the credit of the Colony by loan; taxation; postal service; trade; commerce; fisheries, etc. The Government is also the custodian of the public funds, from which are disbursed the expenses of the various public services.

There are at present eighteen electoral districts, sending thirty-six members to the House of Assembly. The voting is by ballot, and manhood suffrage is now established by law. The Governor, who is also Commander-in-Chief in and over the Colony and its dependencies, has the power, in the Queen's name, to commute the sentence of a court of justice; to summon, open, prorogue, and on occasions dissolve the local Parliament; to give or withhold assent to, or reserve for the Royal consideration, all bills which have passed both Chambers. The Legislature must meet once a year. In reality, the electors govern the country, as they choose the members of the Assembly, who, by their votes, maintain in office or overthrow the Government of the day. The Governor may be said "to reign but not to rule." He is supposed to act in harmony with his responsible ministers, unless in some special cases in which he may consider the principles of the Constitution or Imperial interests to be imperilled.

On the whole, responsible government has worked well in Newfoundland; and under it the country has made great and substantial progress. The boon of self-government, by which the people obtained the power of making their own laws, expending their revenue, and guiding their own affairs, was to them of immense value, and, once granted, it could never be permanently withdrawn. It might be abused, and even attended by heavy drawbacks, but the preponderance of advantages was altogether in its favour. It has proved to be a most valuable school for developing the intelligence and energies of a free people, and promoting national progress.

It is no doubt true that here, as in Canada and most of the self-governing Colonies, a certain price had to be paid for liberty. The freedom that has been long denied, when at length granted, is apt to have an intoxicating effect, and is almost certain at first to be abused. Such was the result here, but not to a greater extent than in the Lower Provinces and Canada under similar conditions. The years which followed the introduction of representative government were, at election seasons especially, marked by strife and bitter contentions, leading to social discord, and at times to scenes of turbulence and disorder; but the area of such troubles was but limited, and they speedily subsided after the elections were over. They remind one of scenes which occurred in England at election times in the first quarter of the century, when party violence was rife. Here, too, it must be remembered, the population of the Colony was composed of two great bodies differing in race and religion, as was the case in Canada. Nearly half of the inhabitants were Catholics of Irish descent, among whom, it might naturally be expected, memories of old-world strifes, wrongs and oppressions would be rife. The other half were

Protestants of English and Scotch descent, who had been accustomed to hold the ascendency. These were headed by a wealthy mercantile class, who were not disposed to give up their time-honoured claim to rule. When, then, representative government came, it is not wonderful to find that old jealousies and distrusts were revived, and that each party dreaded the political supremacy of the other. Hence too often political excitement ran high; and in some cases outrages were perpetrated by the ignorant and turbulent, which added fuel to the flames.

Happily these are now things of the past—mere temporary brawls which subsided after a short time, and over which the judicious historian will draw the veil and consign the memory of them to oblivion. Gradually both parties learned, by bitter experience, the folly of such proceedings and the serious injuries thus entailed. Each learned to respect better the rights of the other, and to recognize the equality which the constitution established. Kindlier feelings were restored, and old strifes were forgotten. Not that these discords disappeared in a day; but as intelligence spreads and higher feelings are called into play, they will disappear for ever.

The introduction of vote by ballot has had a most salutary effect in securing quietude at election seasons, and in preventing any undue influence being employed to interfere with the freedom of voting. After the storm has subsided the waves continue for a time to roll; and so with political storms, the turbulence of the waves subsides only gradually.

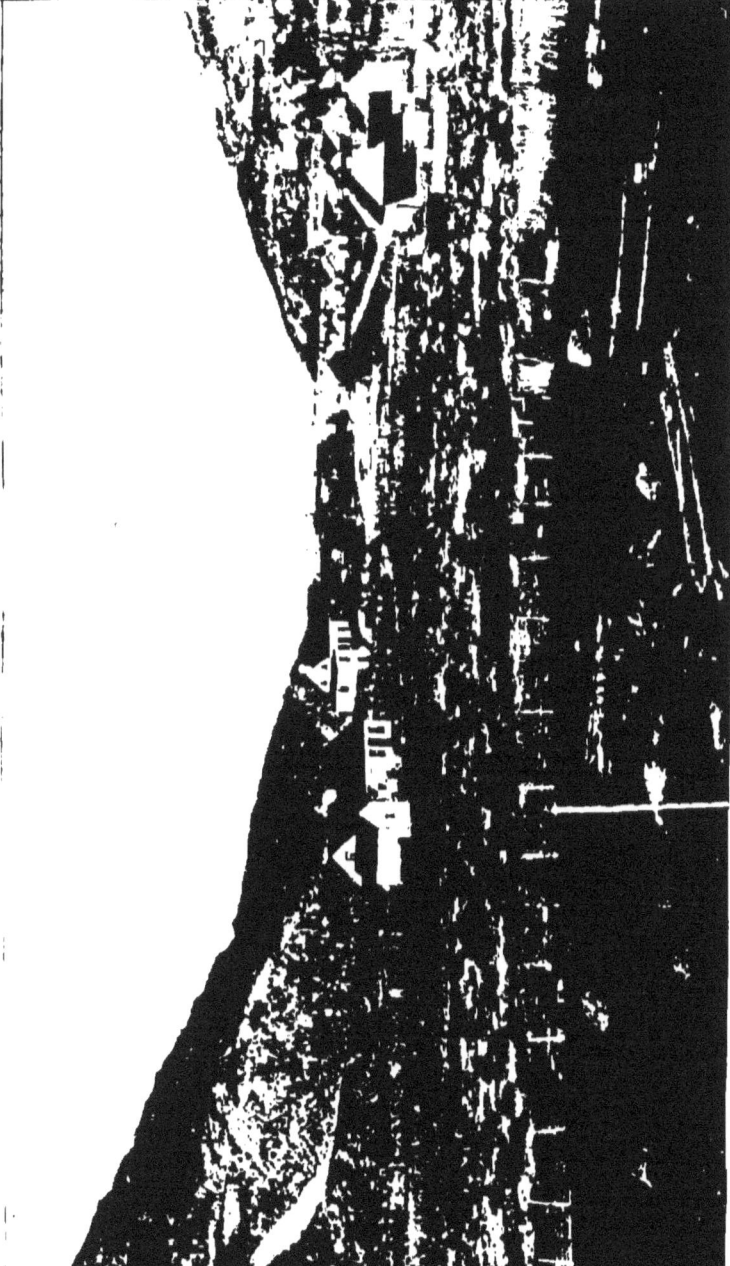

PETTY HARBOUR, SOUTH OF ST. JOHN'S.

This much, too, may be truly affirmed—that the intelligent men of all parties are now of one mind as to the danger of having uneducated masses of men exercising the right of electing by their ballots members of a Legislature; and hence that a more thorough education of the whole people is essential to the safety and well-being of the commonwealth. It is no doubt true that—

> "The crowning fact,
> The Kingliest act,
> Of Freedom is a Freeman's vote."

But it is equally true that it is all-important that the voters should be possessed of intelligence and integrity, if they are to wisely control and protect the liberties and the life of the country. The call for universal education is emphasized by the boon of universal suffrage. The safety of the State demands it. Those into whose hands power has now passed must be educated in order that they may use that power wisely, otherwise society may be overthrown. Democracy is everywhere steadily advancing. Statesmen, aristocracies, middle classes, moneyed classes, are all called upon to make note of the fact that big-fisted, broad-shouldered Democracy has arrived. This rough Frankenstein of the nineteenth century has enormous power for good or evil; and the interest of every community consists in educating it, warming its religious faith, purifying its morals, and inspiring it with a reverence for law, justice, and religion. This is especially true of Newfoundland; and it is gratifying to note that the Legislature has made a liberal provision for the education of the people, and that already a great improvement is visible.

JUDICATURE.

The Supreme Court was instituted in 1826 by the promulgation of a royal charter. To it and to magistrates belong the correct interpretation and proper enforcement of the laws of the country. The Supreme Court is composed of a Chief Justice and two assistant judges. There is also a court of Labrador, with civil and criminal jurisdiction over such parts of Labrador as lie within the government of Newfoundland. There are district courts for St. John's and Harbour Grace. Courts of general and quarter sessions are held, and are presided over by the stipendiary magistrates and justices of the peace.

THE CONSTABULARY AND FIRE DEPARTMENT.

For the detection and prosecution of law-breakers and the preservation of the public peace, a constabulary force is maintained. It consists of an inspector-general, a superintendent, a chief inspector and district inspectors, head-constables, sergeants, constables, and nine mounted police. The total force numbers one hundred and twenty-one. It was first organized after the withdrawal of the military in 1871, and was modelled on the famous Royal Irish Constabulary, being in every respect disciplined and equipped as they are. It is a very fine body of men, and performs its duties most efficiently. Of the whole force, forty-seven constitute the St. John's staff, and the rest are distributed in Harbour Grace, Carbonear, and the various outposts. It is maintained at a cost of $56,000 per annum. Properly speaking, it is a military as well as a civil force, being carefully drilled in the use of arms.

Last year, on the appointment of Mr. John R. McCowen, a most zealous and efficient officer, to be Inspector-General, the constabulary force underwent a thorough reorganization, which has greatly increased its efficiency; while its usefulness has been extended by combining it with the Fire Department, which is also under the direction of the Inspector-General. The city of St. John's is divided into three police districts, each having a station, and the officers and men of each are responsible for the peace and good order of their respective precincts. Telephone communication is maintained day and night between the three stations, and also the police office. The system has been modified somewhat, and made an exact counterpart of the Royal Irish Constabulary, which is admitted

NOTE.—Mr. J. R. McCowen, Inspector-General of Newfoundland Constabulary, is an Irishman by birth, and the son of a British army officer. He served nine years in the Royal Irish Constabulary with distinction, and on retiring from the service received very high credentials from his superiors. In 1871 he was appointed to the Newfoundland Constabulary, and rendered valuable aid in its organization, especially in connection with the mounted force. Afterwards he was promoted to the governorship of H.M. Penitentiary. His management of that establishment elicited the highest commendation. He is now promoted to the important post of Inspector-General of Constabulary; and the Fire Department is also placed under his control. In his new position he has again displayed his genius for organization, and greatly increased the efficiency of both the constabulary force and fire brigades.

to be unsurpassed in efficiency. The semi-military character of the force is apparent in its organization, uniform, equipment, and discipline. The most competent judges have conceded that the discipline, physique, and general tone of the whole force will bear comparison with any similar department on the continent of America. Such eminent authorities as Commodore Curzon Howe and Sir Herbert Murray have spoken in commendatory terms of the management of the constabulary force.

But perhaps the Inspector-General, Mr. J. R. McCowen, has rendered a still more important service by his admirable reorganization of the Fire Department in St. John's after the great fire of 1892. The city is divided into three fire districts, each having its station fitted with all modern improvements necessary to complete a first-class fire department. Everything is automatic that can be made so. The horses become free by means of a simple pull. The harness is suspended directly over each horse's place in front of the engines and hose-reels, and is automatically dropped on their backs. Each horse knows his place perfectly well, and rushes to it the moment the alarm is given. The firemen sleep in the dormitory above the apparatus floor, with everything so arranged that the moment the gong sounds they can be out of bed, dressed, and on their way to the fire in the short space of forty seconds. Cases have occurred in which from the moment the alarm was given until the firemen and apparatus were at the scene and had water playing on the fire, only four minutes had elapsed. The newest and most approved "Gamewell" Fire-Alarm Telegraph System is employed, and gives unqualified satisfaction.

The total force numbers 124 men. There are 13 horses, 45 "Gamewell" alarm boxes, 3 steam engines, extension ladders, gongs, etc. The men are paid, volunteer fire-brigades being discarded. The total cost to the citizens per annum is only $9000—a very moderate amount. The brigade protects about thirty millions' worth of property, only one-third of which is insured. It is believed that there is not anywhere, in proportion to its size, a more efficient and complete fire department. It is the boast of Inspector-General McCowen that in fifteen minutes from the sounding of an alarm he can have 150 fire-fighters on duty. As the benefits of this service are felt in arresting fires and reducing the destruction of property by conflagrations, the rates of insurance will be reduced by the fire insurance companies, whose profits will be increased by an extension of insurance at more moderate rates than at present. The general prosperity of the community will also be advanced, through the confidence and security inspired by these improved fire-defences.

Post-Office.

The postal service, under the direction of the present energetic Postmaster-General, J. D. Fraser, Esq., has been brought to a condition of great efficiency, and compares not unfavourably with that of any other British Colony. The post-office in St. John's is fitted up with all modern improvements, and the building itself, with its various arrangements, is creditable to the Colony. A parcels post with the United Kingdom, the United States, and Canada is of great advantage to the community. There is also an inland parcels post. The book post, post cards, stamps, post-office boxes, money orders, letter carriers, present every facility that could be reasonably desired, and prove that this service is managed with a view to the wants of the general public. The total number of post-offices in the Colony is forty-six. Postal communication between St. John's, the United Kingdom, and European countries, the United States, and Canada, is maintained by various lines of steamers. Communication with the outside world is regular and frequent. On the completion of the new railway, there will be a tri-weekly mail.

LIGHTHOUSES.

The coast of the island is well lighted, and almost every year witnesses an increase of lighthouses and other means of securing the safety of its large seafaring population. At present there are thirty-nine lighthouses and beacons maintained by the Newfoundland Government, and nine by the Canadian Government. There are three fog-signals and one whistling buoy at the most dangerous points around the coast under the Newfoundland Government, and seven fog-signals at the Canadian lighthouses. The erection of most of these has been the work of the last fifty years—a sufficient proof of progress in that time.

BANKS.

The Savings Bank is a Government institution, and it is enacted by statute that "the general revenue of the Colony is liable for all moneys deposited in the bank, and all interests payable thereon." This gives absolute security to depositors. The rate of interest is three per cent. The deposits at present amount to about $1,300,000, and are steadily increasing. The other Banks are "The Bank of Montreal," "The Bank of Nova Scotia," and "The Merchants' Bank of Halifax."

THE NEWSPAPER PRESS.

The following newspapers are published in St. John's:—the *Royal Gazette*—weekly; the *Evening Telegram*—daily; the *Evening Herald*—daily; the *Daily News*—daily, also a weekly issue; the *Enterprise*—weekly; the *Trade Review*—fortnightly; the *People*—monthly; the *Centenary*—monthly.

The following papers are published elsewhere:—*Harbour Grace Standard*—weekly; the *Twillingate Sun*—weekly; the *Trinity Record*—weekly.

CHAPTER X.

FINANCES OF THE COLONY.

Newfoundland's Revenue—Rate of Taxation—Public Debt per Head: how Represented—State of the Revenue at Present—Retrenchment Policy—Late Commercial Crisis: Rapid recovery from—Financial Condition at the Close of 1896—Reforms.

NEWFOUNDLAND is a free-trade Colony. Its revenue is almost entirely derived from customs duties on imports, only a small proportion arising from Crown lands, light dues, and the postal service. The duties on imports are partly *ad valorem*, and partly specific, but only to a very slight extent differential, the tariff being designed for revenue purposes only, not protection. All expenses for such matters as making and repairing roads, bridges, breakwaters, public wharves, etc., are defrayed out of the public revenue, the Board of Works having charge of this department. The provision for the poor, for education, for the maintenance of the police force, for the administration of justice, and for the whole Civil Service, is also chargeable on the general revenue.

The following figures show the condition of the revenue since 1887:—

THE NARROWS AND HARBOUR OF ST. JOHN'S.

Year.	Revenue.
1887	$1,272,600
1888	1,370,030
1889	1,362,893
1890	1,454,536
1891	1,820,206
1892	1,883,791
1893	1,753,845
1894	1,641,035
1895-96	1,564,457

If we take the revenue of 1895-96, $1,564,457, and the present population as 210,000, we find that there is a taxation of $7·44 per head for the entire population: It must be remembered, however, that there are no direct taxes in the Colony except a municipal tax in St. John's for water, light, sewerage, and street improvements, which is but small. This amount of $7·44 *per capita* represents almost the whole amount of taxation. In the United Kingdom the taxation is $6·62 per head; in New South Wales, $12; in Western Australia, $22; in New Zealand, $16·91; in Canada, $5·81. But in all these countries there are direct taxes, in addition, and in some of them these are onerous, and greatly swell the total amount of taxation. Newfoundland, therefore, compared with other colonies, must be regarded as a lightly-taxed country.

The following figures show the amount of the funded public debt in the years named:—

Year	Debt.
1887	$3,005,040
1888	3,335,589
1889	4,133,202
1890	4,138,627

Year.	Debt.
1891	5,223,364
1892	6,393,367
1893	8,255,546
1894	9,116,535
1895-96	13,096,945

The increase in the public debt has arisen mainly from the construction of between six and seven hundred miles of railway. These lines of railway, as was shown in a previous chapter, were absolutely necessary for opening up the interior of the island and developing its agricultural, mineral, and forest resources, thus providing for the expansion of an increasing population. Without a railway all the rich natural resources of the country must remain dormant, and the Colony sink into a condition of stagnation. But that such an investment will yield excellent returns, and add to the wealth of the country, and increase its revenue, cannot be doubted. In previous pages ample proofs of this have been furnished. The public debt is represented not only by the lines of railway which belong to the Colony, but also by the St. John's Dry Dock—one of the largest in the world—which cost $600,000; by the new post-office, a very creditable building, and by various other public works, such as roads, lighthouses, breakwaters, bridges, etc.

If we take the public debt at the close of the fiscal year, June 30th, 1896—$13,096,945—it amounts to $62 per head of the entire population. This is moderate when we compare Newfoundland's indebtedness with that of other Colonies, as the following figures will prove :—

COLONIES.	DEBT PER HEAD.
New South Wales	$240
South Australia	300
Tasmania	245
Cape of Good Hope	8C
Natal	65
New Zealand	285
Queensland	350
Dominion of Canada	49·78
Victoria	200
Western Australia	190

In the United Kingdom the debt is $86 per head; in Belgium, $63; in France, $146; in Italy, $75.

Thus, both in regard to taxation and its public debt, Newfoundland compares favourably with any other Colony.

Then when we turn to the condition of the revenue, we find ample assurance that in railway construction and other public works the Colony has not gone beyond its means, and can well afford to pay the interest on its debt without any undue strain. Within twenty years the revenue has doubled without any great increase of the tariff; and judging by the experience of the past, there is every reason to anticipate a steady increase of revenue in the future.

On the close of the fiscal year, June 30th, 1896, the revenue showed a surplus of $206,492; and this amount, together with the unexpended balance of the late loan, amounting to $360,000, has been placed at interest; so that the sum of $566,492, bearing interest at 3 per cent., is now at the credit of the Government, and is available to meet any emergency that might arise. This shows that the Colony is perfectly able to shoulder its debt, and that no difficulty whatever will be experienced in meeting the interest on that debt, as well as all other charges on the revenue. The estimated revenue for the year ending June 30th, 1897, is $1,587,221, being $22,918 in excess of the revenue for 1895-96. The first six months of the current fiscal year have yielded a revenue of $800,000; so that there is a strong probability that the anticipated surplus will be exceeded.

Perhaps the best guarantee for the stability of the financial credit of the Colony is the fact that in 1895 a policy was adopted by the Government, involving a judicious retrenchment of expenditure in the various public services, without at all impairing their efficiency. This was found perfectly practicable, and was firmly carried out, with the best results. The effect has been to accomplish a saving in the public expenditure of $564,000 per annum—more than enough to cover the entire interest on the public debt, up to the present date. No more important step was ever taken by any Government of this Colony than this retrenchment of expenditure. As is the case under all popular Governments, there had been in the past a tendency to a lavish and careless expenditure, and an indifference to making income and expenditure balance each other, when any deficit was easily met by a loan. The retrenchment, which had become necessary, has placed the finances in a thoroughly satisfactory condition. This, combined with the sound and healthy condition of the revenue, has stabilitated thoroughly the public credit abroad. Trade and commerce have also felt the benefit; and confidence being restored, enterprise and activity have been awakened.

The retrenchment policy had become a matter of necessity in consequence of the severe commercial disasters which overtook the Colony at the close of 1894. On the 10th of December in that year the only two banks in the country—the Union and Commercial —whose notes constituted almost the entire currency, closed their doors, entailing widespread ruin and leaving the community without any circulating medium. The crisis was of the most alarming character. Stores and shops were deserted, for the people had no money to purchase goods. Ruined shareholders were bemoaning their losses; noteholders looking in despair at their worthless paper, which had no purchasing power; and depositors stunned at the discovery that their funds had disappeared. Employers were compelled to close their workshops and factories, having no means of paying wages, and no customers for the products of their industry. Long-established mercantile firms were falling day after day. To crown all, a run on the Savings Bank—a Government institution—commenced, and continued to increase in volume. Men's hearts were failing them, for all confidence was gone. The revenue began to decline as importations fell off. Commercial and industrial chaos had seemingly arrived. The condition of the two defunct banks was, on examination, found to be hopeless.

Nothing shows the thorough commercial soundness of the Colony, and its marvellous recuperative energies, more than its almost complete recovery from this financial collapse within a single year. In reality its vital powers were untouched by the disaster that seemed at first overwhelming. Its people faced their difficulties with a spirit and gallantry that merited the highest praise, and they came off conquerors. In a single year after the crisis nearly all traces of the havoc wrought by the financial storm had disappeared. The old Colony, that had been thrown on its beam ends in the tempest, had righted itself, and was sailing onward prosperously. Business had revived; the wheels of commerce were revolving vigorously; money was plentiful; the various industries were in full activity; three Canadian banks, of the first class, had replaced the defunct local banks, and the whole tone of trade and commerce was buoyant and hopeful. The Hon. Robert Bond, Colonial Secretary, on behalf of the Government, had skilfully negotiated an advantageous loan by which the floating debt had been provided for, and the Savings Bank had been rendered safe in any emergency, by another loan of a million dollars. The revenue had been restored to a healthy condition, and at the end of the year showed a surplus. A judicious policy of retrenchment, already referred to, had effected an annual saving of $564,000. Credit abroad and confidence at home were restored. The contrast between the December of 1894 and that of 1895 was astounding.

Another year passed, and at the close of 1896 the economic condition of the Colony was found to have still further improved. Recovery had proved to be permanent. Progress was steady and continuous. The trade and commerce of 1896 were of a satisfactory nature. The fisheries were above an average, and industrial enterprise, in many directions, was active. Credit had been curtailed and business more largely conducted on a cash basis. The revenue still continued to advance, and the Government were able to show a surplus of $206,493 over expenditure.

In point of fact, the effect of the commercial crash of 1894 has been to reform abuses which had crept into the commercial system, and to place business on a sounder basis than before. The main cause of that financial disaster had been the dangerous and vicious system of banking on which for years the business of the country had been conducted. These banks had furnished undue facilities of obtaining credit—in some cases to an enormous extent—and this led to an inflation of trade. Their capital was thus swallowed up. In such a condition of affairs a slight matter would precipitate a crisis, which at length arrived. All this is ended. The improved banking methods introduced by the Canadian banks has told favourably, and placed monetary affairs on a sounder basis than before; and while all due facilities are furnished by these banks for a legitimate business, all wild and speculative schemes are steadily discouraged.

Another still more important reform has been introduced. The supplying, or truck system, on which the fisheries have been carried on, has received its death-blow. It was the cause of evils innumerable; and though it will not altogether disappear for some time, it has been greatly curtailed. The "crash" has been far from an unmixed evil. A country that has so quickly recovered from its effects must have a future before it.

CHAPTER XI.

Scenery of the Island: the Norway of the New World—Health resort: the Summers — Attractions for Travellers and Tourists — Novelty of the Scenery—The Fishermen—Professors Bickmore and Hyatt on the Character of the Scenery and Climate—Captain Kennedy's Testimony—Archbishop of Halifax: his Experience— The London *Times* on Newfoundland—Sport and Angling— Grouse-shooting—Deer-stalking.

NOT many years have elapsed since the discovery was made by the outside world that Newfoundland contains some of the grandest and most beautiful scenery that the traveller can find in any land. Formerly, the idea of associating "the land of fog and cod-fish" with the sublime and beautiful in Nature would have been scoffed at. All that was known about the island was summed up in Burns' lines in his "Twa Dogs"—

"Some place far abroad,
Where sailors gang to fish for cod."

The prevalent idea was that it was mostly shrouded by a curtain of fog, and that the interior was a region of dismal swamps and naked rocks. Gradually these mistaken ideas have been dispelled; and now every year witnesses an increasing number of visitors from the outside world—tourists in search of the picturesque and beautiful, travellers, health-seekers, sportsmen—

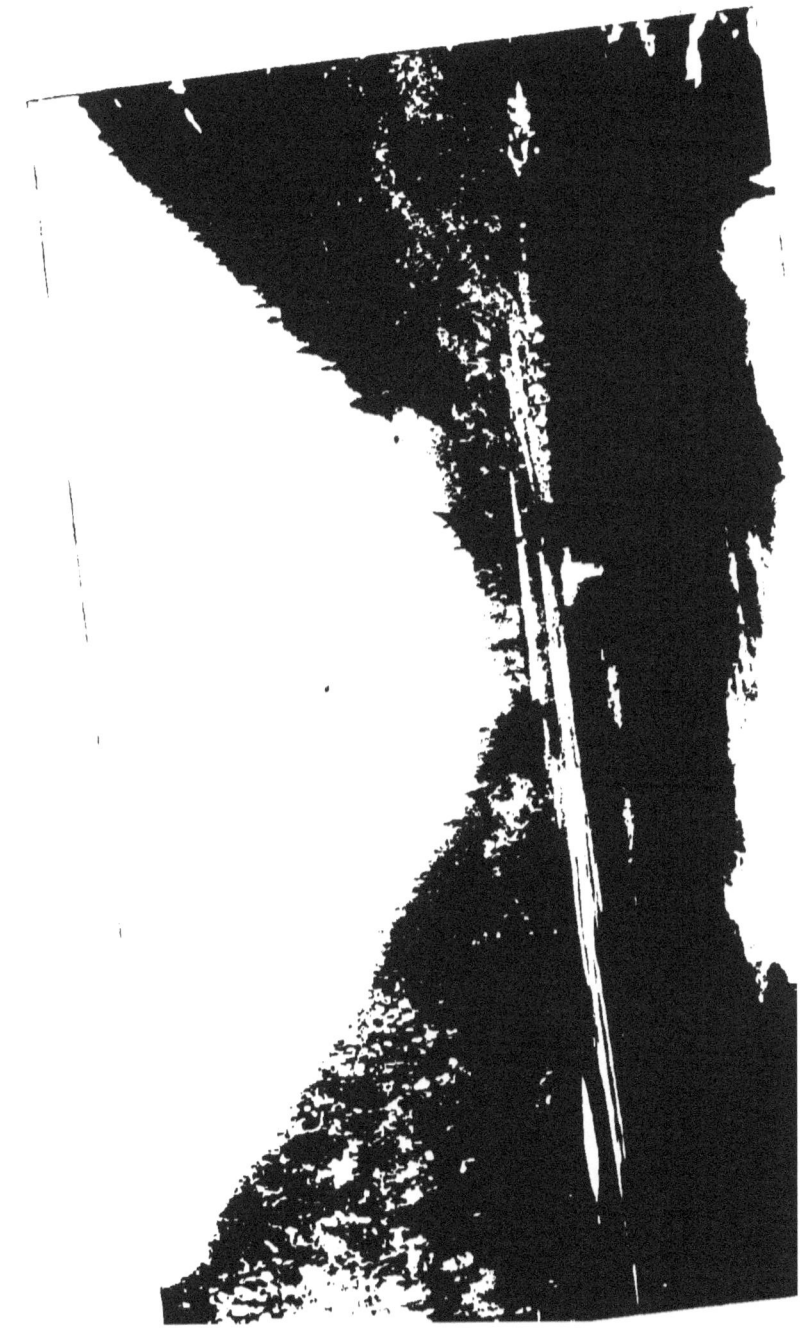

who carry back with them glowing reports of the wonderful attractions of this "gem of the Western world."

Newfoundland has been well named "the Norway of the New World." In many points it strikingly resembles that country to which tourists flock from all lands. Its deep fiords which indent the shores, everywhere guarded by lofty cliffs, whose forms are reflected in the clear bright waters of the bays, have a remarkable resemblance to those of Norway, and are frequently not less magnificent in their scenery. Many of these great watery ravines, running inland for eighty or ninety miles, and exhibiting a wonderful variety of scenery along the great arms which they project in all directions, are on a grander scale than the famous Norwegian fiords. The great bays of Trinity and Placentia, which almost cut the island in two, have no parallel in respect of size among the Norwegian fiords. Then, in their short but beautiful summers, their bright skies, their exhilarating atmosphere, their population of fishermen—so abundant in insular peculiarities and primitive characteristics, hidden away in nooks remote from all the outer world, quaint in manners, gracious to strangers—the two countries resemble each other very strikingly. Norway was once as little known as Newfoundland, and its natural beauties as little appreciated. Now it is the resort, each summer, of many hundreds of travellers, and, by its fine system of roads, it has been rendered everywhere accessible. Another point of resemblance is that the inhabitants of both countries are noted catchers of cod and herring, and have long been rivals in the Spanish and Mediterranean fish-markets. Norway has long had the start of Newfoundland in regard to its scenic attractions for tourists and travellers; but the turn of the Norway of the New World has come at length. The artist and the photographer have been at work, and pictorial illustrations of its scenery—of which the pages of this volume contain some specimens—are making it widely known, and thus the stream of visitors is swelling.

As a sanitorium—a health resort—Newfoundland is destined to take a high place, when the accommodations and comforts which travellers or invalids require are provided—as unquestionably they will be—at the most desirable places throughout the island. Here the people of the United States and Canada will find a welcome escape from the burning heat of their own summers. They will enjoy scenery novel and attractive; a bracing, exhilarating air that imparts new vigour to the frame, and sends back the smoke-dried citizens with freshened complexions and the tide of health coursing through their veins. In summer the heat is never oppressive, and the nights are always cool; so that, after a day's ramble, sleep comes sweet and refreshing. There is something peculiarly balmy, soothing, and yet invigorating in the summer breezes, whether on sea or land, cooling the fevered brain, and smoothing the wrinkled brow of care. After a few weeks near the coast, inhaling the sea breezes, and exposed to the life-giving rays of the sun, the invalid who has come with shattered nerves and fluttering pulse will generally return with a new supply of iron in his blood, and a sense of well-being which makes it a luxury to live. With the completion of the new railway to Port-au-Basques, the island will be rendered easy of access to travellers, who, embarking at Sydney, Cape Breton, in a luxuriously appointed steamer, will in five hours be landed on the shores of Terra Nova. There a number of summer weeks can be spent climbing the rocky heights of the New-land; wandering over its plains, bright with wild flowers; plying the angler's rod, or bending the oar in the clear water of its countless lakes; stalking the lordly caribou, or shooting the ptarmigan (superior to the grouse) over its "barrens" and hills; or exploring the great fiords which stretch their arms far inland, amid the wildest and grandest scenery. All this to the denizens of the smoky, dust-laden cities is like passing into a new and brighter state of existence, and enjoying for a time a purer and better life.

One thing the tourist may safely reckon on is the sensation of novelty. Not only are the aspects of Nature, indeed, the whole character of the scenery, such as are not commonly met with elsewhere, but here the traveller finds himself among a new race of people— the hardy fisher-folk, quaint in their manners, having their own ways of looking at things; entirely unaffected by the conventionalities and fashions of the outside world; primitive in their modes of living; kindly and friendly. Travellers will find such archaic people abundantly interesting, and worthy of a careful study. They are original, quaint, and in many ways quite unique.

Travellers who have visited the country have in

numerous instances borne testimony to its attractions. An eminent American professor—Albert L. Bickmore, of New York—after a short tour in the island, wrote of it: "In regard to beauty and grandeur of scenery, health-giving climate, and general attractiveness for those whose energies have been lowered by city life, and who seek to recuperate, few countries could surpass Newfoundland. Many hundreds of Americans would every year find their way here were the country only known. In future, if proper steps are taken, Newfoundland may become one of the most popular summer resorts. In addition to the scenery and pure air, you have salmon and trout fishing to an unlimited extent; and in the fall, snipe, curlew, and ptarmigan shooting, as well as deer-stalking. Boating on the lakes; driving or walking over the breezy hills; picnicing in such places as Petty Harbour, Middle Cove, or Topsail; sketching or photographing the rare scenery; drinking in the oxygen of an atmosphere which at every breath quickens the pulse and puts colour in the cheek—what more could the heart of man or woman tourist ask for?"

Professor Hyatt, of Boston, one of the most eminent geologists of America, spent three months with a party of scientists on the west coast, engaged in searching for fossils. He wrote of his excursion in the following terms: "Certainly one can rarely see in this world more remarkable and picturesque villages than those of Burgeo, Burin, and Rose Blanche. The effect of the pond-like harbours, surrounded by rugged hills, often of considerable height, is rendered exceedingly pleasing, often lovely by the habit of building the cottages anywhere and everywhere, according to the fancy and fortune of the owner. Burgeo was especially remarkable, and an artist could spend many summers on its coast, and become its pictorial historian with great gain to himself." The professor found Port-au-Port "a geological paradise," and curious fossils most abundant. "I have one *endoceras*," he wrote, "two feet six inches long, and with the living chambers nearly perfect—one of the finest things I have ever seen in any collection, not even excepting Hall's or Barrande's. We also found abundance of fossils at Ingornachois Bay, where the fossil cephalopods are marvellous in size and number. We have revelled for ten days with hammer and chisel in digging these out." Of the west coast the professor wrote: "The weather favoured us in Newfoundland. We were not detained by fogs, and had very few adverse winds. The scenery was superb, and has made all the countries we have passed through since seem tame and unpicturesque, except, indeed, the steep mountainous cliffs of Cape North, and the vicinity in Cape Breton. I can never expect to get so much pleasure, combined with intellectual profit, out of any future trip." "From St. George's Bay to St. John's Island, on the western coast, the mountain ranges form a series of steep cliffs, cones, and domes, which also greatly enhance the beauty of the deep and branching fiords of Bay of Islands and Bonne Bay. The climate, vegetation, and lovely harbours make the trip along this part of the route a series of delightful surprises."

Captain Kennedy, R.N., formerly commander of H.M.S. *Druid*, who spent several years in Newfoundland, published some dozen years ago "Sporting Notes on Newfoundland." The following are extracts from this interesting work:—" To one who, like the writer, has had the opportunity of seeing the country, of mingling with its warm-hearted inhabitants, of penetrating into the vast and almost unknown interior in quest of sport, Newfoundland presents a deeply interesting aspect, whether it be from a sporting, an artistic, or a social point of view." "The fogs on the east and south coasts seldom if ever penetrate inland; and I have no hesitation in saying that for four or five months in the year, namely, from June to October, inclusive, *the climate is far superior to that of Great Britain;* while the winters are undoubtedly milder than those of Nova Scotia, Canada, or New Brunswick. During the months of July, August, September, and part of October, the weather is magnificent, the thermometer ranging occasionally as high as 85°. At this time the country presents a most beautiful appearance, resembling in parts the Highlands of Scotland. The mountains are clothed to their tops with many kinds of woods, conspicuous among which are the fir, maple, birch, and hazel. The 'barrens' are covered with a rich carpet of moss of every shade and colour, and abound in all sorts of wild berries, pleasing both to the eye and taste. The banks of the rivers are also at this time fringed with wild strawberries, raspberries, currants, blueberries, and adorned with many kinds of lovely ferns and wildflowers; while foaming torrents and tumbling cascades complete a picture delightful to the eye of the artist and the salmon-fisher. The scenery of the south coast is of the grandest description : deep gorges in the coast-line lead through narrow entrances, with precipitous cliffs on either hand, to magnificent harbours, where the navies of Europe may float secure from every gale." " In the interior of the island are thousands—ay millions—of acres of good land, suitable for growing crops, or raising cattle or sheep, as shown by the magnificent wild grasses which grow in all the swamps, and upon which the deer feed unmolested, save when the solitary hunter intrudes upon their sanctuary. As regards salubrity of climate, Newfoundland has no equal. On our visits round the coast the doctor's duties were absolutely *nil*." " I believe that few countries have such advantages as are possessed by Newfoundland, with her magnificent harbours and her boundless stores of wealth : but no country has ever yet progressed without railroads or even roads. With the completion of the railway to the west coast; with copper mines in full blast along her shores, and other industries in like activity, the proud boast of every Newfoundlander— 'This Newfoundland of deers'—will be no idle one, and the sovereignty of the island will be assured not only in name but in reality." (The foregoing was written twelve years ago. It will be seen that Captain Kennedy's anticipations are receiving a rapid realization.)

The late Roman Catholic Archbishop of Halifax paid a visit to Newfoundland a few years ago. In a published description of his trip he wrote :—" It is strange how ignorant we are of the beauties and attractions of places near our shores, while thoroughly conversant with the lesser grandeur of historic lands far away. Thousands from the United States and many from Canada yearly flock to Europe, and write rapturous accounts of the scenes over which poetry or fiction has thrown a glamour. For a trifling outlay, and without the discomforts of a long sea-voyage, they could, by visiting Newfoundland, enjoy a cool and healthy summer, and revel in all the wild grandeur of Alpine scenery, or dream away the hours by lakes and bays compared with which Killarney and Loch Katrine are but tame and uninviting pools." "You find yourself in a land where the virgin forest still fringes the noblest bays in the world; where the codfish actually swim within a yard of the shore, and salmon bask in the ledges of secluded inlets."

Some sixteen years ago, when Newfoundland was much less known than at present, the London *Times*, in an article calling the attention of travellers and tourists to this island, used the following words:—" Newfoundlanders can doubtless exist without the constant intercourse of Englishmen. But they not unnaturally take a little umbrage at being let down, in pure ignorance, through being left out of the track of British tourists, as a population resembling, in locality and habits, the Esquimaux. Canada and the Cape and Natal, and even the sequestered Shetlands, have each for its especial class of taste and imagination, its traits of peculiar interest and fascination. They have at all times had their delights and graces remarked. Newfoundland alone

HUMBER RIVER (NEAR ENTRANCE).

has been left to the chance of one or another of its people caring to expatiate on its merits, and being so importunate or skilful as to gain an audience. Were but a single trial given, to borrow the language of advertisers, the British public is assured that Newfoundland would soon become a favoured resort. It is guarded by as many terrors and obstructions as if it were the cave of a dragon and his treasure. Yet behind the barrier of cloud and ice lies a land of pleasant airs and radiant sunshine. There are woods and meadows and flowers. There are cathedrals and concert-rooms and libraries, with all the luxury attendant upon dwellers in villas." . . . . . " Newfoundland as a Colony is dwarfed by its relation to two continents as a central fish-market. For itself it has promising mines which would reward capital and enterprise, were not both monopolized by the hereditary pursuit. It has fertile belts which will bear wheat in profusion. It has vast expanses of practicable pastures. Railways will open up tracts of agricultural territory which are now presumed to be irreclaimable marshes and wildernesses. In the meantime there is hunting as good as in the great American North-West, without the distance to travel, and with hospitality and friendly English fellow-citizens to welcome the sportsman. What is wanted is just a little sunshine and countenance from the mother-country to stir the islanders themselves to develop Newfoundland for Newfoundlanders. Life is easy, yet not too easy. Nature affords a sufficiency of opportunities without enervating the population by doing its work herself. Travellers who have the courage to penetrate the veil of fog and winter, and the more obstinate barrier of discouraging presumption of perennial gloom, will discover that life is worth living among Newfoundland balsam poplars; and that the oldest English Colony has with age only deepened and intensified its English characteristics."

After sixteen years it is pleasant to know that the anticipations of the great English journal have been fully verified, and that Newfoundland is every year attracting greater attention. The external rocky ramparts of the island are apt to be repellant to the passing voyager; but within these frowning outworks, up the great fiords, with their countless branches, along the banks of the rivers and brooks, among the rolling hills, and over the great "barrens," are scenes of rarest beauty; and over all, in summer, is a sky blue and serene as that of Italy, and more varied in its changing aspects. No element of Nature's sublimity and beauty is wanting. In drives or rambles along the shores of bays, the road now scales the lofty hills, then dips down into silent dells, and ever and anon breaks out to the sea through wood-skirted ravines. There, in the distance, are the glittering icebergs sailing majestically past; or here, aground in some quiet cove, lies one of the white wanderers, the waves gently laving its sides, while cascades are pouring from its summit as it melts under the fierce rays of the summer's sun. Everywhere the eye is greeted with some new fantastic form of cliff or rich colouring of porphyry rock; while the softness of delicate mosses contrasts at intervals with the ruggedness of bare rocks on which the gnawing tooth of Time has been operating for countless ages. At almost every turn of the road little gem-like lakes flash into view, their waters clear as crystal, many of them with moss-clad islets sleeping in their bosoms. Such a drive in a bright summer's day around these great sea-arms is something to be remembered to the close of life.

It does not come within the scope of this little volume to refer at any length to the sporting attractions of the island. In the author's "Hand-Book and Tourists' Guide" (Kegan Paul) full information will be found. To lovers of sport, few other countries present greater attractions. Its countless lakes and lakelets abound with trout of the finest description, and are the homes, in summer, of the wild goose, the wild duck, and other fresh-water fowl. The willow ptarmigan (*Lagopus albus*), the rock ptarmigan, the curlew, the plover, the snipe are found, in the proper season, all over the island, on the great "barrens" or in the marshy grounds in immense numbers. The sea-pigeons and guillemots are all around the shores and rocky islands. The Arctic hare is met with, and the North American hare is abundant. Above all, the noble caribou, or deer, in vast herds traverse the island in periodical migrations from south to north, and furnish the highest prizes for the sportsman. The rivers contain the lordly salmon and the finest trout. For the more adventurous sportsmen there are the black bear and the wolf in the interior; while the beaver and otter are found in the lonely lakes and ponds. Here is a paradise for sportsmen. Newfoundland could readily be made the finest deer-park in the world by passing and enforcing laws for the protection of its deer.

CHAPTER XII.

Geographical position of the Island—Its importance—Bays—Coastline — Population — Saxon and Celtic elements — Education: Schools, Colleges, Scholarships—Higher Education—Educational Grant—Religious Denominations—Social aspects—Condition of the People.

THE geographical position of Newfoundland is singularly important and commanding. Anchored at no great distance off the North American Continent, and stretching right across the entrance of the Gulf of St. Lawrence, to which it affords access at both its northern and southern extremities, it might be regarded as a place of arms and defence; for the Power which possesses it holds the key of the St. Lawrence. Its south-western extremity is within sixty miles of Cape Breton Island; while its most eastern projection, Cape Spear, near St. John's, is but 1640 miles distant from Ireland. Thus it is adapted by Nature to serve the peaceful interests of commerce, and to facilitate intercourse between the Old World and the New.

In another aspect it might be considered as a huge bastion thrown out from the shores of the Dominion of Canada, which, if duly fortified, might become the Gibraltar of these Northern seas.

In another respect the hand of Nature has marked the island as a centre of commercial activity. A glance at the map shows that its coasts are pierced by numerous magnificent bays, running in some instances eighty or ninety miles inland, and throwing out smaller arms in all directions. In these deep bays are some of the finest harbours in the world. They bring with them the marvellous fish-wealth of the surrounding seas, and place it within reach of the fisherman's net and hook. To such an extent are the shores indented that, though the island is about a thousand miles round, measuring from headland to headland, its entire coast-line is considerably more than double that extent of mileage. In fact, it would be difficult to find anywhere an equal land-area, presenting such an extent of frontage to the sea. It ranks tenth in size among the islands of the globe, being 216 miles in length, and about the same in breadth, with an area of 42,000 square miles. It is almost equal in size to the Empire State of New York; it is twice the size of Nova Scotia, one-sixth larger than Ireland, three times as large as Holland, and twice as large as Denmark. Hitherto only its sea-margin has been utilized; but now that the interior has been pierced by railways, and its resources rendered accessible, it may be truly said that 42,000 square miles of territory have been added to Britain's Colonial Empire by the new railway system.

The population of this great island is at the present day only about 210,000, including the residents on Labrador. Now that the hinterland is opened up for settlement, and a splendid field for mining enterprise made accessible, it may be reasonably anticipated that the next ten or twenty years will witness a large increase of population. When the best lands along the line of railway can be purchased for thirty cents per acre, when forest lands can be had for lumbering at a low rate, and when mining is extending rapidly and various new industries taking root, it will not be long ere Newfoundland will attract no inconsiderable rill from the great emigration current that is constantly flowing westward past its shores.

The present population of the island has come of good stock, being derived entirely from the Saxon and Celtic races. Moreover, the blood in this isolated region has been kept free from any undesirable intermixtures; and so far this blended race has been developed under favourable circumstances. The intermingling of Saxon strength, energy, and endurance with Celtic swiftness, brilliancy, and emotional activity, ought to produce a superior race, having the best qualities of the stocks from which they originated. The proportion in which the two races stand to each other, according to the last census, was—Saxon, 129,354; Celtic, 72,696.

Thus on the side of Newfoundland, the tough, enduring Saxon, and the more lively, versatile Celt, have met in not very unequal proportions; and from this wholesome amalgamation of races have sprung the stalwart men and comely matrons and maids whom the traveller of to-day looks on with admiration. The race has taken kindly to the soil, and thriven. Living in one of the most salubrious climates in the world, breathing an invigorating atmosphere, engaged largely in open-air employments—many of them constantly battling with the billows—a hardy, energetic race has grown up, well fitted for the world's rough work. They and their fathers have buffeted the waves, and drunk in the health-giving sea breezes; and now we find the present generation of Newfoundlanders, in their general physique, a powerfully-built, robust, and hardy race.

An excellent system of education has been established on the denominational principle, each religious denomination receiving a *per capita* allowance from the State in proportion to its numbers. The people have learned to appreciate the importance of education, and great improvements have been effected within the last twenty years. There are now about 560 elementary schools, attended by about 36,000 children. The higher education is provided for by four institutions connected respectively with the four different religious denominations. These have expanded and greatly elevated the standard of education, and are now designated "colleges," and are known as the Church of England, the Roman Catholic, the Methodist, and Presbyterian Colleges. Pupil teachers are trained in these colleges; and pupils are prepared for the universities.

St. John's has been made a Colonial centre of the London University, so that pupils can here prepare for and pass the matriculation examinations. Openings are thus provided for the more talented and aspiring of the young to attain distinction, and fit themselves for the higher posts of duty. A scholarship has been founded this year—value $500 per annum—in commemoration of the Queen's Diamond Jubilee. A "Council of Higher Education" has been established with a view of promoting a higher standard of education throughout the Colony, by the holding of examinations, and the awarding of prizes, diplomas, and scholarships to successful candidates. It is composed of representatives of all the denominations. The Legislative grant for colleges and elementary schools is $151,891; or *per capita* about 75 cents. All travellers are struck with the mental quickness and general intelligence of the people; and now that education is doing its work, it will be found that here is a people who, when duly cultured, will play no unworthy part in the world of the future, and will be able to compete with the brain-workers of the coming age in all departments of life. The people are a law-abiding, orderly race. Serious crime is rare, and the proportion of offenders against the law, in proportion to the population, is very small. They are quiet, church-going, warmly attached to their religious faith. They live peaceably among themselves, and outbreaks of bigotry and fanaticism are almost unknown.

The following figures show the respective strength of the religious denominations according to the census of 1891:—

Church of England	69,834
Roman Catholic	72,696
Methodist	53,276
Presbyterian	1,449
Other Denominations	4,795

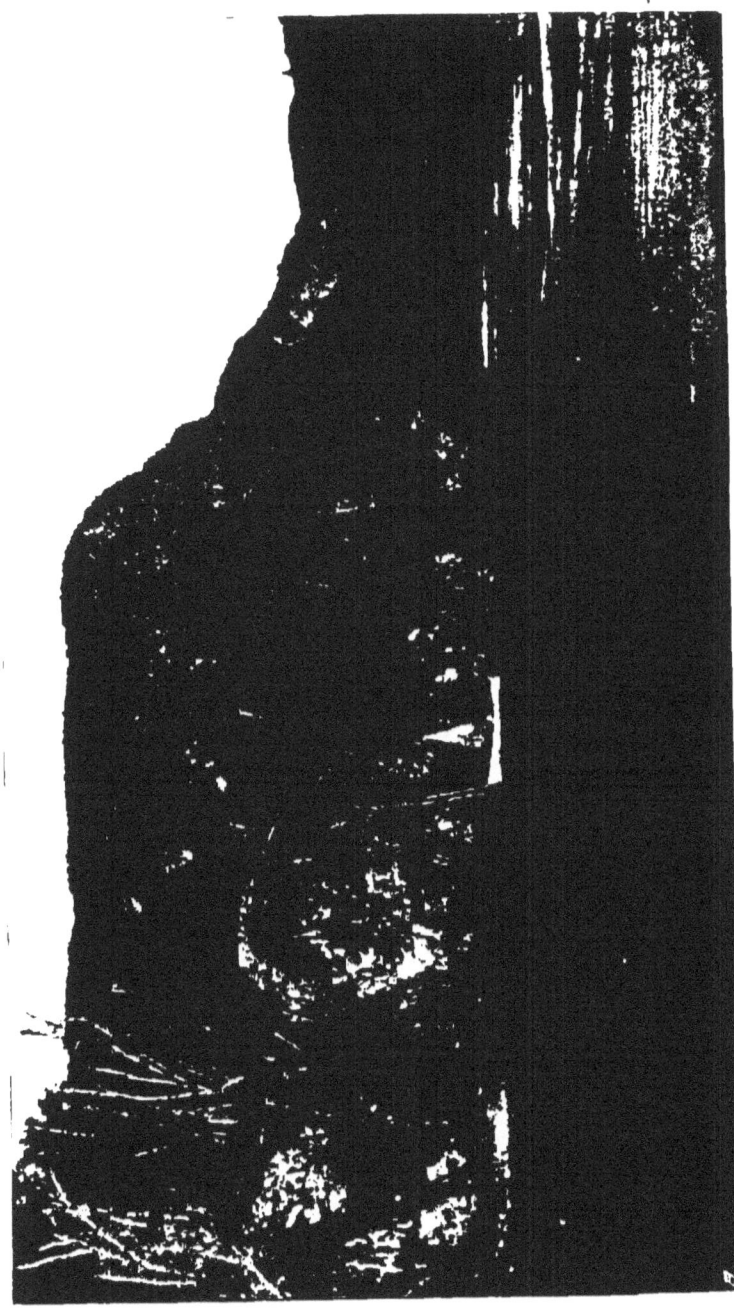

DEVIL'S DANCING POINT, HUMBER RIVER.

There is, of course, no distinction of ranks other than that arising from wealth, education, or official or professional position. The upper-class is composed of the officials of the Government, members of the Legislature, judges, clergy, merchants, doctors, lawyers, and wealthy individuals who have retired from business. The middle-class is composed of the newer merchants, importers, commission agents, shopkeepers, tradesmen, farmers, and that large class who by industry and economy have acquired a modest competence. It is among this middle-class that the sentiment of progress has taken deepest root, and that a strong desire for the development of the resources of the island is most keenly felt. The fishermen and the working classes generally welcome the prospect of new industries for the support of themselves and their children, feeling that the fisheries alone are insufficient for their increasing numbers. Late years have witnessed a marked improvement in the condition of the fishermen. They are becoming more provident, and far larger numbers of them than formerly can now afford to dispense with supplies on credit at the beginning of the fishing season, and pay in cash for what they require, thus buying their necessaries at a much cheaper rate. Those who combine farming with fishing are invariably the most independent and comfortable of their class. On the whole, the fishermen of Newfoundland, though they have not much of this world's goods, compare not unfavourably, as to their condition, with the labouring classes of other countries. If they have privations and hardships, they have compensations for these in their free, open-air life, their robust health, their capabilities of enjoying simple pleasures. There is perhaps as genuine happiness among them as among any similar number who toil for their daily bread. Their passionate attachment to the land of their birth, their love for it when settled in other countries, and their frequent longings to return, all indicate that their life on the whole has been a happy one.

CHAPTER XIII.

Influence of the New World on the Old—Great Duel between England and France for Supremacy in North America—Its Bearing on Newfoundland—Treaty of Utrecht—The Beginning of Troubles—Evils of Concessions to the French—Misinterpretation of the Treaties—Their Injury to the Colony—Lobster Difficulty on the Treaty Shore—Delegation to the House of Lords—Best Policy for the Colony.

IN the great duel between England and France for supremacy in North America, which extended over a century and a half, the French made many attempts to obtain entire possession of Newfoundland. They were fully aware of the strategic importance of an island which commanded the entrance to the Gulf of St. Lawrence and their possessions in Canada, and which would also enable them to control the valuable fisheries. Hence they never ceased in their efforts to obtain a footing in the island, and their presence and encroachments were a constant source of annoyance to the settlers.

In earlier chapters we have pointed out the vast results which followed from the discoveries of the Cabots, and the hold which England thus obtained on the soil of North America. The reflex influence of the

New World on the Old changed the whole current of European politics, and affected deeply the fortunes of the leading nations of Europe. Five great nations— England, France, Spain, Portugal, and Holland— struggled for more than a century for a share of these vast territories. More and more England concentrated her efforts to gain possession of North America, and in doing so laid the foundations of that "Greater Britain" beyond the seas which from Queen Elizabeth to Queen Victoria has been steadily expanding. Her great rival was France. Very early some of the ablest statesmen of France saw the vast importance of these new lands, and determined to establish a dominion worthy of the great name of France. No expense was spared in promoting the growth of Colonies which would give the French a firm hold on these magnificent possessions. Able and wise governors were appointed; soldiers for defence were furnished; food was supplied in seasons of scarcity. In this way, year after year, "Greater France" extended itself along the banks of the St. Lawrence. Quebec and Montreal were founded. From the great lakes the French pushed their discoveries and explorations down the Mississippi to the Gulf of Mexico, and claimed the enormous territory drained by it and its tributaries. But meantime English colonization was extending itself rapidly along the shores of New England. These colonists were men of brave hearts and strong arms, and possessed of a free, bold spirit. It is not wonderful that Colonies planted by such men soon attained a robust growth. Very soon they discovered that unless the ambitious designs of France were checked they would be hemmed in on north and west, and perhaps driven from their possessions. They began to extend themselves northward in order to secure the valuable Canadian fur trade. This the French would not tolerate; and so the great duel between the two races began. At a later date they met in the valley of the Ohio, where the French prohibited the English colonists from trading. England came to the assistance of her Colonies, and war commenced with the view of expelling the French from the American Continent.

The French fought with great bravery in defence of their possessions. In Newfoundland they made desperate efforts to obtain possession of the island. At an early date they had firmly established themselves in Placentia, which they fortified strongly, and also seized on other places along the southern shore. An English force was despatched against them, and several of their settlements were destroyed, and the fortifications at St. Pierre were demolished; but they still kept possession of their stronghold Placentia. From it they made repeated raids on the English settlements, burning and destroying. At length, in 1708, they despatched a force from Placentia, in the middle of winter, which surprised the unprepared garrison in St. John's, and captured the place. They attacked Carbonear, but were repulsed. Meantime, however, the fortunes of war went sadly against the French elsewhere, both on the Continent of America and in Europe. The military power of France was broken, and Louis XIV. was glad to accept peace on very disadvantageous terms. The war was brought to a close by the Treaty of Utrecht, 1713.

This treaty marks a new era in the history of Newfoundland. It stipulated that "the Island of Newfoundland, with the adjacent islands, should belong of right wholly to Great Britain"; but, unhappily for the peace and prosperity of the Colony, it also stipulated that it shall be allowed to the subjects of France "to catch fish and cure them on land on that part only of the coast" defined in the treaty; and that "it shall not be lawful for the subjects of France to fortify any place in the said island of Newfoundland, or to erect any buildings there besides stages made of board, and huts necessary and usual for drying of fish, or to resort to the said island beyond the time necessary for fishing and drying of fish."

This was the beginning of troubles for the unfortunate colonists of Newfoundland, which have gone on till the present hour, and are now as far as ever from being settled. It is true the power of France in the New World was gradually weakened, and that, one after another, their strongholds were captured. At length their last battle was fought on the heights of Abraham, in 1759, where the gallant Wolfe "died happy," and Quebec was captured. This was one of the decisive battles of the world; and after it the white flag of France no longer waved on the Continent of America. Still they clung to the idea of conquering and holding Newfoundland; and three years after, in 1762, a naval squadron was despatched from Brest, which surprised and overpowered the small garrison at St. John's, consisting of but sixty-three men, and took the city. Their triumph was short-lived. When the news reached Halifax, Lord Colville, with Colonel Amherst, were despatched with a strong force. They landed their troops six miles from the city, marched overland, and stormed Signal Hill, a lofty eminence overlooking the harbour, which was held by the French in considerable force. The French fleet in the harbour managed to escape in a fog, but their garrison surrendered. This was the last attempt on the part of the French to gain possession of the island.

But though the French were worsted in the battlefield, they proved themselves to be masters in diplomacy, a department in which England has never excelled. The hold they had acquired by the Treaty of Utrecht they never relinquished. On the contrary, by some mysterious influence which they wielded, in 1763, when the Treaty of Paris was concluded, they obtained an addition to the previous concession; the King of Great Britain then " ceded in full right to His Most Christian Majesty the islands of St. Pierre and Miquelon" (in the mouth of Fortune Bay) " to serve as a shelter to French fishermen; and His Most Christian Majesty engages not to fortify the said islands, to erect no buildings upon them, but merely for the convenience of the fishery, and to keep upon them a guard of fifty men only for the police." These conditions have been entirely disregarded by the

French, who have made St. Pierre a Colony, and erected buildings of all sorts. The Treaty of Versailles, 1783, confirmed the previous treaties, and attached a "declaration" which introduced new complications.

Little did the British statesmen, who were responsible for negotiating these treaties, foresee the endless worry and trouble to which they were to give rise between the two nations—often endangering their peaceful relations; and as little were they aware of the cruel injuries and injustices they were inflicting on the patient, toiling colonists. It is indeed totally impossible to understand the motives which prompted them to consent to such a preposterous arrangement. The islanders had suffered sorely from the presence of the French for over a century. The Treaty of Utrecht gave British statesmen a fine opportunity to free this long-suffering Colony for ever from their presence. Instead of doing so, they fastened the French grasp on the island more closely by granting them fishing privileges, and ceding to them two islands close to the shore.

Look at the disastrous results to British interests! The French have placed an interpretation on the language of the treaties which it does not bear, and which both the colonists and the Imperial authorities repudiate and refuse to admit. The French have all along insisted with the utmost pertinacity that the terms of the treaties secured to them an *exclusive* right to the use of the fisheries; so that British fishermen could neither lawfully fish within these limits, nor occupy the land for any other purpose.

THE DUNGEON, BONAVISTA.

The coast-line to which these treaties apply extends from Cape Ray, at the south-western extremity of the island, around the western, northern, and north-eastern shores to Cape St. John—almost half the island, and, in regard to soil, climate, forest, and mineral wealth, by far the best half of the island. The effect of these treaties has been to practically exclude the people from the fairest half of their own territory; to prevent the investment there of capital in industrial enterprises. Had it not been so locked up, it would long since have been colonized, and a farming, fishing, lumbering, and mining population would have been in occupation, with thriving towns and villages along its entire extent.

Thus to the Colony these antiquated treaties, the work of Imperial statesmen, have been most injurious, and have retarded its progress more than all other causes put together. No such wrong has ever been inflicted on any other British Colony. In addition, St. Pierre and Miquelon became smuggling centres, to the great loss of Newfoundland's revenue.

England and her subjects, the colonists, refuse to admit the *exclusive* claim of the French, and have always maintained that they had a *concurrent* right, provided they did not "interrupt" the operations of French fishermen. This was Lord Palmerston's view, and also that of the Crown lawyers of England.

In 1889 a new and very serious complication arose. Some twelve thousand British subjects are now settled on this treaty shore, some of whom have years ago commenced the new industry of canning lobsters. The

French, witnessing their success, also commenced lobster canning; and not only so, but preferred an exclusive claim to the lobster fishery, and used active measures for the removal of British lobster factories. This flagrant disregard of the provisions of the treaties roused public indignation in the Colony, and a strong agitation commenced, which ended in an appeal to the English people and Parliament. The local Legislature finally sent a delegation, who claimed to be heard at the Bar of the House of Lords, and this rare privilege was granted. It was a memorable historic scene when Sir William Whiteway, as Premier of the Colony, addressed that august assembly, setting forth the long array of his country's grievances. The appeal of the delegates was heard with deep sympathetic interest, and Parliament and the Press of England joined in admitting the justice of the position assumed by the delegation. The end of it was that a *modus vivendi* was arranged, and has been renewed and prolonged till the close of 1898. The object is to allow of negotiation, and, if possible, secure arbitration regarding the vexed question.

It is not wonderful that the colonists keenly feel the injustice of shutting up one-half of this fine island in order that a few French fishing vessels may use it at certain points for drying their fish during three or four months in the year.

But then existing facts must be looked in the face. France has again and again declared, through the mouth of her foremost statesmen, that she will not accept a money compensation for these treaty rights, or even a territorial exchange. The national sentiment will not permit it. English statesmen have spared no pains to bring about a settlement, but in vain.

What, then, is the wisest policy for Newfoundland to adopt? The colonists, by their temperate presentation of their grievances, have won the sympathy of England and the respect of her leading statesmen. They may rest assured, then, that as soon as an opportunity presents itself their wrongs will be righted. But England cannot accomplish impossibilities. She cannot disregard her treaty obligations; and she has no power to compel France to forego her treaty rights. Surely, then, all right-thinking men will agree that the duty and interest of the Colony lie in co-operation with the Imperial authorities, both in securing a proper measure for the enforcement of the treaties, and also in the settlement of the whole question in the future. The present time calls for moderation, self-control, and the exercise of that good sense which will calmly look facts in the face.

Whatever may have been the conduct of the Imperial-Mother towards the oldest of her Colonies in the dark days of the past, she has now for her eldest-born nothing but the kindest intentions and the most sincere goodwill. In this Jubilee Year such friendly feeling has been evinced in the invitation of all the Premiers of the self-governing Colonies to share in the commemoration of the sixtieth anniversary of Her Majesty's reign. It is a recognition of the Colonies as a part of her ocean-empire. It is a pledge that if any one of them is suffering a wrong, it will be considered and put right. If, then, Newfoundland colonists will, in this complicated trouble connected with French treaty rights, be patient and wise, while firmly holding on to their rights, the day is not distant when all present difficulties will admit of an easy solution.

APPENDIX I.

THE GREAT SEAL-HUNT OF NEWFOUNDLAND.

PANNING SEALS.

IN the North Atlantic there are two great rivers ceaselessly flowing—one warm, the other cold. The former is known as the *Gulf Stream*, the latter as the *Arctic Current*. They form an important part of that grand movement of circulation in the waters of the ocean which is just as essential to the life and well-being of our planet as the circulation of the blood in the maintenance of the vitality of the human body. A constant interchange of the cold polar and the warm equatorial waters is going on, and is all-important in the economy of the globe. Strange as it may seem, every drop of water in the ocean passes slowly and gradually from the poles to the equator and back again, and from the greatest depths up to the surface; and this is absolutely essential to maintain the balance of Nature. There is a gradual creeping flow of the polar waters towards the equator, along the floor of the ocean, caused by the difference in temperature; and to compensate this movement, the lighter and warmer equatorial waters are constantly floating towards each polar region, thus modifying the heat of the one and the cold of the other.

But in addition to this vertical circulation there are the better-known superficial movements of the ocean waters, in horizontal directions, constituting the currents or great rivers of the ocean. These are largely caused by the trade winds in each hemisphere, and may be regarded as supplying streams necessary to complete the vast oceanic circulation. One of these is the Gulf Stream. By the pressure of the equatorial streams, a great "head" of warm water is formed in the Gulf of Mexico, from which it escapes by the narrows of Florida, the momentum carrying it northward along the coast of the United States as far as the Banks of Newfoundland, where it is deflected eastward, and merging itself in the general drift of the ocean, it flows north-easterly, adding itself to the warmed waters carried by this drift-current past the British Isles and Norway into the Arctic Gulf between Spitzbergen and Novaya Zemlya.

The counter-current to this warm stream is known as the Arctic current. The great volume of water driven into the Arctic Gulf, as described, escapes mainly by the ice-bearing current of East Greenland, which sweeps round Cape Farewell, flows north as far as Cape York, and, being here deflected westward, it mingles with another escape current coming from the Arctic regions through Baffin's Bay and Davis's Strait. It now flows south, and, receiving a fresh accession from Hudson's Strait, moves along the shores of Labrador and Newfoundland till it encounters the warm waters of the Gulf Stream going eastward. Here it is divided into two parts, one wedging itself between the Gulf Stream and the American coast, the other shooting under the warm waters of this second river in the ocean. The circulation is now complete. From Labrador southward it is usually called the Labrador current; and the area which it occupies on the coasts of North America is the great feeding and breeding ground of the commercial deep-sea fishes, and of various air-breathing animals. Thus, then, the cold river in the ocean, which bears on its bosom huge ice-argosies and chills the atmosphere of these northern lands, is the source of the vast fish wealth which has been drawn on for ages. Wanting this cold current, the cod, seals, herrings, mackerel, halibut, hake, etc., which now crowd the northern seas would be entirely absent. So far from being unfavourable to the production of animal life, the Arctic seas and the great rivers which they send forth are swarming with life, from the minute diatom and crustacean to the oleaginous seal, the ponderous walrus, and the unwieldy whale.

Among the various forms of marine life to be found in these ice-laden waters, not the least remarkable and commercially valuable is the seal. In the cold waters of the Arctic current it has its *habitat*, and the great ice-fields are essential to its existence. With its coat of fur, padded by thick layers of fat, it is exactly adapted to its surroundings. Amid the floes formed from the thickest Arctic ice it has thriven and multiplied in incredible numbers. On these floes of the Labrador current its young are brought forth, cradled, and suckled. It is in their babyhood that the young of these great seal-herds are brought within reach of the hardy seal-hunters of Newfoundland, who brave all the perils of the ice-wildernesses in pursuit of their prey. These daring men force their way through the crystal ramparts by which Nature has guarded the helpless innocents, and slay them by

PUTTING SEALS ON BOARD.

thousands in their icy cradles. The great annual seal-hunt from the ports of Newfoundland involves a vast destruction of seal-life, young and old, and constitutes one of the most remarkable industries of the world. Its importance to Newfoundland may be estimated from the fact that the value of its annual products ranges from half a million to a million of dollars, and that some six thousand men, twenty-two large steamers, and a number of sailing vessels take part in the seal-hunt. To this must be added a considerable number of men, who are

THE GREAT SEAL-HUNT.

employed in the manufacture of the oil and its preparation for market. All this industry is dependent on the play of those great forces of Nature by which the circulation of the waters of the ocean is maintained.

It should be noted that the seals captured here are not fur seals of Alaska, whose soft coat makes glad the heart of the city belle, but the oil seals. Their skins are used for the manufacture of a coarse-grained but expensive

SCALPING THE SEALS.

leather employed in the making of trunks, boots, purses, etc., and also in costly book-binding. The oil is used for illumination, for lubricating machinery, and for making the finest soaps, and like uses.

There are four species of seals in the waters around Newfoundland and Labrador—the bay seal, the harp, the hood, and the square flipper. The bay seal is local in its habits, does not migrate like the others, but frequents the mouths of rivers and the harbours round the coast, and is never found on the ice. It is mostly taken in nets, but commercially is of small importance. The harp seal —*par excellence* the seal of commerce—is so called from having a broad curved line of connected dark spots proceeding from each shoulder and meeting on the back above the tail, and forming a figure something like an ancient harp. The hood is much larger than the harp. The male, called by the hunters "the dog-hood," is distinguished from the female by a singular hood or bag of flesh on his nose. When attacked or enraged, he inflates this hood so as to cover the face and eyes, and it is strong enough to resist seal shot. When thus protected, he can only be killed by shooting him in the neck and the base of the skull. The dog-hood fights desperately in defence of his mate and young ones, and if they are killed he becomes furious, inflates his hood, while his nostrils dilate into two huge bladders. His appearance is now terrific, and with uncouth floundering leaps he rushes on his foe. Instances have occurred where a fight between an old dog-hood and five or six men has lasted for an hour; and sometimes a hunter is fearfully torn, and even killed, in the encounter. The square flipper seal is the fourth kind, and is believed to be identical with the Greenland seal, and is from twelve to sixteen feet in length. It is only occasionally met with in these seas.

Another circumstance by which the seal industry of Newfoundland is determined is the migratory movements of the seals. These are as regular as the flow of the Arctic current. About the middle of February their young are born on the ice-fields off the north-east coast of Newfoundland. The young are suckled by their mothers for six weeks, and about the 1st of April they take to the water. Early in May they commence their northerly movement in company with their young, shaping their course for the Greenland seas, where they spend three months. As the early Arctic winter sets in with September, they begin their southern migration, keeping ahead of the ice as it forms, and moving towards the coast of Labrador, and feeding in its fiords and bays as they move. Small detachments seem to lead the way, like pioneers. Behind them moves the great army in one continuous mass. It occupies days in passing certain points, and appears to fill the sea as far as the eye can reach. This great army on its march may well impress the beholder with the idea of the vast number of seals, on whose ranks the hunters make their annual onslaughts. Having reached the Straits of Belle Isle, separating Newfoundland from Labrador, one division enters the Gulf of St. Lawrence, the other moving along the eastern shores of the island, feeding in its bays and inlets, but both divisions steadily going south. Towards the close of the year they have reached the Banks, these being their southern head-quarters, as the Greenland seas are their northern. The Banks are ever swarming with fish, and on these the seals feast till the beginning of February; then they commence their northern migration to meet the Arctic ice, on which their young are to be brought forth and cradled. By the 10th or 15th of February they have reached the ice-fields, descending on the Arctic current, and these great floes are the birthplace of their young. Their annual round is now completed.

The great aim of the hunters is to get among the "white-coats," as the young harp seals are called, in their babyhood, when yet fed by their mother's milk, and while they are powerless to escape. The oil, too, extracted from the blubber of the young seals is of a much finer quality than that obtained from the full-grown seals. The milk on which they are sustained is of a thick creamy consistency, yellowish in colour, and very rich and nutritious. This is proved by the extraordinary rapidity of their growth. When born they weigh some six or seven pounds, and in three weeks they have increased to forty or fifty pounds. The baby seal is born with an oily coating of blubber just beneath

WHITE-COAT SEAL.

the skin, which in ten or twelve days thickens from half an inch to three and even four inches.

Formerly the seal-hunt was carried on in stout schooners, but these have been, in late years, almost entirely superseded by steamers strongly built, sheathed with iron-wood, and having their stems plated with iron, so as to cleave their way through the ice-fields. Each carries from two hundred to three hundred men, and these are the *élite* of their class. It would be difficult to find a finer body of stalwart men than the ice-hunters of Newfoundland. Their powers of endurance are marvellous; and their daring courage in battling with the floes and following their prey amid the crashing bergs and ice-masses, from which other men would shrink in terror, shows that they are quite at home in these grim solitudes. The perils and hardships they have to encounter, the skill and courage required in fighting the ice-giants, and the possible rich prizes to be won, lift this adventure above the ordinary level, and throw around it a romantic interest. Not the seal-hunters alone, but the whole population, from the richest to the poorest, take a deep interest in the fortunes of the hunt. It is like an army going out to do battle for those who remain at home. A steamer will sometimes go out and return in two or three weeks, bringing home as many as thirty to forty thousand seals, each worth two dollars and a half. The successful hunters are welcomed with ringing cheers, like returning conquerors, and are the heroes of the hour. What tales they have to tell of perils in the icy wildernesses, of narrow escapes from being crushed, of cold plunges into the treacherous ice-chasm, of fierce combats with the "dog-hoods"! No wonder the young Newfoundlander pants for the day when he will get "a berth to the ice," and share in the wild joys and excitements of the hunt.

Nothing, however, could be more uncertain than the fortunes of the seal-hunt. These vast ice-fields are often from one hundred to two hundred miles in breadth, and of unknown length. The *locale* of the seals depends on the winds and waves. The most skilful sealing captains fail at times to strike the "seal-patches," and not infrequently return to port "clean," or with only a few hundred seals. There are great successes, such as that of the s.s. *Neptune*, Captain Blandford, in 1894. After an absence of eighteen days, she returned to port with every nook and cranny crammed with pelts, and even her decks piled with the oleaginous treasures, till her gunwale was only two feet above the water. She brought in 42,000 seals,

S.S. "NEPTUNE" IN THE ICE.

value about $105,000. For one brilliant success like this there are, however, many costly failures; for the position of the icy cradles in which the young "white-coats" lie is utterly uncertain, and though in searching for them skill and experience count for much, yet "the race is not

THE GREAT SEAL-HUNT. 183

to the swift nor the battle to the strong," but in this case "time and chance happen to them all."

Let us suppose, however, that all difficulties have been surmounted, and that the steamer has at length got sight of the seal-patch. The whimpering of the young seals is heard, gladdening the hearts of the hunters. Their cry has a remarkable resemblance to the sobbing or whining of an infant in pain. No sooner is this sound heard than the vessel is laid-to, the men eagerly bound on the ice, and the work of destruction begins. A blow on the nose from a gaff, heavily shod with iron at one end, fractures the thin skull of the young seal, and in the vast majority of cases it feels pain no more. Death is instantaneous. In a moment the knife is at work. The skin with the adhering fat are detached rapidly from the carcass, which is left on the ice, still quivering with life, though there is no sensation, the movements of the muscles being merely mechanical, and caused by contact with the icy surface. In fact, death comes to the young "white-coats" far quicker and with less pain than to animals slaughtered by the butchers. The pelts, as the skins and adhering fat are called, are then bound up in bundles, and dragged over the hummocky ice to the side of the steamer.

The work of slaughter now goes on without cessation. The hunters scatter over the ice in all directions in search of their prey, and often wander miles from the ship. The ice is soon stained with gore and dotted with the skinless carcasses of the slain. The decks become slippery with mingled blood and fat. Blood-gouts cover the hands and arms of the men. "The shivering seal's low moans" fill the air. What a scene amid these icy solitudes of the ocean, with the bright sun in the heavens lighting up the glittering pinnacles! The poor mother-seals, now cubless, are seen popping their heads up in the small holes among the ice, looking for their snow-white darlings, and refusing to believe that the bloody carcasses on the ice are all that remain of their tender offspring. With a moan of distress they plunge into the sea, as if anxious to escape from the ensanguined trail of the hunters.

Their maternal instinct is peculiarly strong, and the tenderness with which the mothers watch over their

HAULING THE PELTS.

offspring is most touching. When the young seals are cradled on the ice, the mothers go off each morning to fish, returning at intervals to give them suck. It is an extraordinary fact that the old seals manage to keep open holes in the ice, and to prevent them freezing over, in order that they may reach the water. On returning from a fishing excursion, extending over fifty or a hundred miles, each mother-seal is able to find the hole by which

THE GREAT SEAL-HUNT.

she took her departure, and to discover her own snow-white cub, which she proceeds to fondle and suckle, though there may be thousands all around. It is also by the mothers that the young ones are taught to swim. They are seen at times tumbling their babies into the water and giving them swimming lessons. When they are in danger from "rafting ice," or fragments of floes dashed about by the wind, and likely to crush them, the self-sacrificing affection of the mothers leads them to brave all dangers in order to help their young to places of safety in the unbroken ice, sometimes clasping them in their fore-flippers and swimming with them or pushing them forward with their noses. At the end of six weeks the young shed their white woolly robe, which has a yellowish or golden lustre, and then a smooth spotted skin appears, having a rough darkish fur. They now cease to be "white-coats," and become "ragged-jackets."

The perils of the ice-fields are neither few nor small, and the hardships and exposures such as only men of iron could endure. These men are so accustomed to the floes and the sea that they seem to have an absolute contempt for their terrors. They leap from pan to pan, where it would seem a child could hardly be sustained, and think little of passing a night on the ice far from the steamer, going even four or five miles off in their eagerness to slay. Should a fog or a snow-storm set in, there is a terrible risk of losing their way and perishing miserably in these ice-deserts, or of falling through the openings which are covered with the snow as it falls and freezes. Sometimes the field-ice on which they are at work separates without a moment's warning into fragments, and they are floated off, to perish by cold and hunger, unless rescued by a passing vessel. On the whole, however, such are their skill and fortitude, and their knowledge of the movements of the ice, that comparatively few mishaps occur.

The greatest danger of all is when a violent storm rages, breaking up the ice-fields and driving before it the larger floes intermingled with floating fragments of ice hard as granite. Woe to the unfortunate vessel that is exposed to the blows of these ice-giants. When the wild north-easter rises, the great swell of the Atlantic rolling in continuous ridges heaves the pavement of ice on its mighty folds. Speedily, by the upheaving of the waves, the ice-field is broken up into smaller pieces or floes. The whole mass opens and expands, and then the broken fragments are dashed against one another or piled on each other in hummocks, or hills of ice. At times the fragments are lifted high on the swell and flung upon the floe, being piled over each other in layers fifty feet in height. This is called the "rafting" of the ice. The thundering crashes of the ice-giants as they grapple and dash one another to death, combined with the roaring overhead of the blinding snow-storm, make up a scene of awe and terror. Then at times a huge iceberg takes part in the fray, sailing solemnly forward, rending and tearing the ice-field, and scattering its fragments far and wide. Such are some of the scenes amid which the seal-hunters have to gather in "the precious things of the deep." Considering all the perils, it is surprising that fatal disasters are not more frequent, and that so many vessels, year after year, come home unharmed. During the seal-hunt of 1872 one hundred men perished—fifty of them having gone down in a single sailing vessel, called the *Huntsman*. In the same year two steamers, the *Bloodhound* and *Retriever*, were crushed in the ice and sank; but their crews escaped over the ice, after enduring great hardships. In 1896 two steamers, the *Windsor Lake* and the *Wolf*, were crushed in the ice

THE GREAT SEAL-HUNT. 187

in such a storm as has been described, but no life was lost. Three more of the fleet were "nipped" and considerably injured.

These violent storms, happily, are not frequent. For the most part the sea is at rest, and then the ice-fields present a strange beauty of their own, which has a wonderful fascination. The moon, the stars, and the flickering aurora bring out in perfection all their wild

THREE CANADIAN BANKERS ON THE ICE OF ST. JOHN'S, CONTEMPLATING
A YOUNG SEAL FROM A FINANCIAL STANDPOINT.

loveliness. In the calm which follows a storm the seal-hunters often find themselves sailing gently through quiet waters, amid islets of glittering ice, with shining pinnacles and fantastic forms floating for miles around —a scene of weird and fascinating beauty.

When the vessel reaches port with her fat cargo, the skinners go to work and separate the skins and the fat. The former are salted and stored for export. By means of steam-driven machinery, the fat is cut up by revolving knives into minute pieces, then ground finer by a sort of gigantic sausage-machine, afterwards steamed to extract the oil, and then exposed for a time in glass-covered tanks to the action of the sun's rays, and finally barrelled for exportation. The annual catch of seals is from 200,000 to 400,000.

To Newfoundland this industry is of immense im-

FULL-GROWN HARP SEAL.

portance, and, with wise regulative measures, there is no reason why the fishing should not be indefinitely prolonged. At a time when other northern countries are locked in icy fetters and their inhabitants largely in a state of enforced idleness, here is an industry that can be plied by the fishermen of Newfoundland, and by which in a couple of months from half a million to a million of dollars may be won.

APPENDIX II.

NOTES ON CHAPTER II.—SEBASTIAN CABOT.

IN these days when detraction is busy regarding the character and work of Sebastian Cabot, it is worth while to turn to the estimate formed of him by some of the most eminent historical authorities. Bancroft, the distinguished American historian, says: " A new patent was issued to John Cabot (1498), less ample in the privileges it conferred; and his son Sebastian, a native of Bristol, a youthful adventurer of great benevolence and courtesy, daring in conception and patient in execution, a man whose active mind for more than half a century was employed in guiding the commercial enterprise which the nations of the West were developing, and whose extraordinary merits have been recently vindicated with ingenious and successful diligence, pursued the paths of discovery which he and his father had opened." " The career of Sebastian Cabot was in the issue as honourable as its opening had been glorious. He conciliated universal regard by the placid mildness of his character. Without the stern enthusiasm of Columbus, he was distinguished by serene contentment. For nearly sixty years, during a period when marine adventure engaged the most intense public curiosity, he was reverenced for his achievements and his skill. He had attended the congress which assembled at Badajos to divide the islands of the Moluccas between Portugal and Spain; he subsequently sailed to South America under the auspices of Charles V., though not with entire success. On his return to his native land, he advanced the commerce of England by opposing a mercantile monopoly, and was pensioned and rewarded for his merits as the ' Great Seaman.' It was he who framed the instructions for the expedition which discovered the passage to Archangel. He lived to an extreme old age; and so loved his profession that in the hour of death his wandering thoughts were upon the ocean. The discoverer of the territory of our country was one of the most extraordinary men of his age. There is deep cause for regret that time has spared so few memorials of his career. Himself incapable of jealousy, he did not escape detraction. He gave England a continent, and no one knows his burial-place."

J. R. Green, in his "History of the English People," says: "Two years before the great navigator (Columbus) reached the actual mainland of America, a Venetian merchant, John Cabot, who dwelt at Bristol, had landed a crew among the icy solitudes of Labrador. A year later, his son Sebastian, sailing from the same English port to the same point on the American coast, pushed south as far as Maryland and north as high as Hudson's Bay. For a long time, however, no one followed in the track of these bold adventurers."

In "Campbell's Lives of the Admirals," art. Sebastian Cabot, we find the following passage: "If this worthy man had performed nothing more, his name ought surely to have been transmitted to future times with honour, since it clearly appears that Newfoundland had been a source of riches and naval power to this nation from the time it was discovered, as well as the first of our plantations; so that with strict justice, it may be said of Sebastian Cabot that he was the *author of our maritime strength*, and opened the way to those improvements which have rendered us so great, so eminent, so flourishing a people."

John Barrow, in his "Chronological History of Voyages in the Arctic Regions," wrote: "Sebastian Cabot, by his knowledge and experience, his zeal and penetration, not only was the means of extending the foreign commerce of England, but of keeping alive that spirit of enterprise which, even in his lifetime, was crowned with success, and which ultimately led to the most happy results for the nation."

Francesco Tarducci, the foremost of living Italian historians, in 1892 wrote an exhaustive memoir of the Cabots, which, in 1893, was translated into English and published. He has carefully gone over all the documents connected with the lives of both, with much critical skill; and he has triumphantly vindicated Sebastian from the only serious charge ever made against him. This author, in closing his memoir, wrote: "We know nothing of when or where he died, nor even the spot where he was buried. England, wholly occupied in coursing the seas over which he had directed her, had no time to remember or mark the sepulchre of the man to whose powerful initiative she owes the wealth and power which have placed her among the foremost nations of the world. What is still worse, her historical literature, so rich in quantity and quality, has not a book in which his life and work are investigated and studied profoundly, and at as great a length as possible, although her writers have at times proclaimed his greatness and protested the gratitude due to him from the English nation."

Henry F. Brownson, the translator of Tarducci's work, says in his preface: "Cabot had been for years looking for land to the West, led by a course of reasoning similar to that which influenced Columbus, and had Columbus never lived, would have been Columbus. Columbus and Cabot looked for a land of gold and spices. Columbus found the lands rich in precious metals, and the result there has been four centuries of cruelty, slavery, and oppression, of despotism and anarchy. Cabot found a land whose only wealth was the cod-fish that swarmed on its coasts; but that land became the cradle of liberty and justice, of resistance to tyranny and oppression, the refuge of the enslaved and down-trodden of every clime. The world—humanity is better, nobler, happier for the discovery made by Cabot. Has any real benefit to mankind resulted from the lands south of us?" . . . .

"It is further claimed for Sebastian Cabot that to him is due the commercial greatness of England; and, if so, of course also of the United States. Moreover, he was the first to propose and to attempt to solve the great problem of the North-West Passage—a problem which may yet remain unsolved till the next century; but to which we owe some of the most sublime examples of heroism and endurance the human race can boast of. Columbus stands on a solid pedestal as the greatest of the world's discoverers; but Traducci claims for the Cabots a rank above all others except Columbus himself; and it is most conformable to the fitness of things that the same author should have written the life of all three."

"After the great Genoese, no one," says Traducci himself, "has such an equal claim to be remembered and celebrated at these centenary festivals as John and Sebastian Cabot."

APPENDIX III.

CABOT COMMEMORATION.

THE author of this volume claims the honour of having been the first to call attention to the fourth centenary of Cabot's discovery of North America, and to urge its celebration. In a paper on "The Voyages and Discoveries of the Cabots," read before the Historical Society of Nova Scotia in 1893, he pointed out the immense service rendered to England by these great navigators, while not the smallest tribute had ever been paid to their memories; and urged that the fourth centenary of their discoveries—in 1897—presented a favourable opportunity of retrieving the injustice of the past and honouring their memories. Subsequently he addressed a letter to the Royal Society of Canada, of which he has the honour to be a Fellow, on the same subject. The Society at once took up the matter, and appointed a committee to make arrangements for a Cabot celebration. In many other places the proposal was received with warm approval. At a later date it was well received in England. The original proposer has thus the satisfaction of seeing his idea, which of course may have occurred to other minds, likely to be carried into practical effect. As far as he is aware, he is the first to put it before the public in tangible shape.

APPENDIX IV.

THE MISSION TO DEEP-SEA FISHERMEN.

THIS noble institution, a few years ago, extended its operations to Labrador. F. J. S. Hopwood, Esq., C.B., C.M.G., now Assistant Secretary to the Board of Trade, paid a visit to Newfoundland some six or seven years ago. He was a member of the Committee of the Mission to Deep-Sea Fishermen; and his report to them of the condition of the fishermen on Labrador, and the hardships and neglect they had to bear, induced them to send out Dr. Grenfell, who has since conducted the Labrador branch with the greatest energy and efficiency. He has built two well-equipped hospitals on that dreary coast, and procured the services of a trained nurse for the management of each. These have been the means of doing an immense good among the poor fishermen, mitigating sufferings, and saving many lives. Dr. Grenfell spends each summer in visiting the scattered settlements along that coast in his yacht, attending to all cases of sickness and others requiring surgical aid, and distributing clothing and food when needed among the more necessitous. He is regarded as an angel of mercy by these poor people, among whom are many women and children, exposed to cold and terrible hardships, and previously without any proper medical aid. It would be difficult to find anywhere a Mission so admirably conducted, or accomplishing so much in mitigating human woes.

It is not wonderful to find that Her Majesty the Queen takes a deep interest in this Mission—especially the Labrador branch—and has lately given it the right to use the title "Royal," by which henceforth it will be known.

INDEX.

A

Agricultural products of Newland, 75
Agriculture in Newfoundland, 104-107
Aldery Brook, 99
America, found by the merchants of Bristowe, 1497, 15, 16; Spain, etc., 8, 48. *See also North America.*
Amerigo Vespucci, 4
Amherst, Col., 167
Amsterdam, foundations of, 41, 112
Arctic current, the, 113-115, 173-176
Arctic exploration, Sebastian Cabot, the pioneer of, 30
Asbestos, 75, 88, 97, 98
Atlantic cable, the, 75
Ayala, Pedro de, Spanish envoy, and John Cabot, 21, 25

B

Baccalaos (New Fish Lands), Sebastian Cabot and, 30
Bacon, Lord, and the Newfoundland fisheries, 57, 58
Badajos, conference at, attended by Sebastian Cabot, 31
Baltimore, Lord, 59, 60
Bancroft, the historian, on Sir H. Gilbert, 49, 51; on John Cabot, 189

Banks, in Newfoundland, 135; failure of two, in 1894, 141-143
"Barrens," 104, 150
Barrow, John, on Sebastian Cabot, 190, 191
Basque Provinces, fishermen of the, off Newfoundland, 43, 44
Bay of Islands, 87, 93, 100, 149; herring fisheries at, 88, 121; marble beds at, 102
Bays round the Newfoundland coast, 157
Bay seal, the, 177, 178
Beauclerk, Lord Vere, 70
Beaudoin, Abbé J. D., on Cabot's landfall, 32, 33
Belle Isle, iron ore in, 94-96
Bennett, Mr. Chas. F., 91 n.
Berry, Sir John, 66
Bett's Cove, copper mine at, 90
Beurinot, Dr., on Cabot's landfall, 32, 33
Bickmore, Prof. A. L., on the scenery of Newfoundland, 148
Biddle and Sebastian Cabot, 26
Blandford, Captain, of the *Neptune,* 119, 182
Bloodhound, s.s., loss of, 186
Board of Works, 136
Bonavista, 109
Bonavista, Cape, said to be Cabot's landfall, 22
Bond, Hon. Robert, 142
Bonne Bay, 93, 149
Bradley, Thomas, 9
Brevoort, on Cabot's landfall, 33
Bristol, John Cabot sails from, in

the *Matthew*, 1-7; his return to, 15; monument to Cabot at, 16
British American fisheries, value of, 113
British maritime enterprise, John Cabot the founder of, 8, 9
British Museum, Privy Purse accounts at, 17
Brittany, fishermen of, off Newfoundland, 42, 44
Brownson, Henry F., on the Cabots, 191, 192
Broyle, Cape, gold-bearing quartz reef at, 100, 101
Burges, village, 148
Burin, village, 148

C

Cabot, John, sails from Bristol in the *Matthew*, and discovers Newfoundland, 1-7, 11-17, 18-20, 32, 40; Sir C. R. Markham on, 8, 9; monument to, 10, 16, 31; ancient writers on his discovery, 19-21; landfall of, 22-25, 32, 33; Henry VII. and, 16, 17, 25; his second voyage, 26, 27; his son Sebastian, 27-29; Bancroft, the historian, and, 189; J. R. Green on, 190; fourth centenary celebration, 193
Cabot, Sebastian, memoir of, by Mr. J. F. Nicholls, 9, 10; monument to, 10, 16, 31; Hakluyt on his papers, 21; map of 1544, 25; early historians on, 26-29; enters the service of Spain, 30, 31; pensioned by Edward VI., 31; his death in London, 1557, 31; Bancroft and other writers on, 189-192; fourth centenary celebration, 193
Cabot Strait, 86
Calvert, Sir George (Lord Baltimore), 59, 60
Campbell's "Lives of the Admirals," article on S. Cabot, 190

Canadian Banks in Newfoundland, 142, 143
Canadian fisheries, value of, 113
Canadian Government, lighthouses maintained by the, 134
Canadian Petroleum Co., 103
Cape Bonavista, said to be Cabot's landfall, 22
Cape Breton (Cabot Strait), 86, 147, 149
Cape North, 25, 149
Cape Breton Island, said to be Cabot's landfall, 22-25, 32, 33; the French and, 42, 43
Carbonear, 131, 165
Caribou, the (deer), 155
Carter, John, 9
Catholics in Newfoundland, 127, 128
Cattle, value of, in 1895, 106
"Cavo Descubierto" (Cape Breton Island), 25
Centenary, the, 135
Charles I., Act issued by Star Chamber of, 66, 67
Chesapeake Bay, 57
Chidley, Cape, said to be Cabot's landfall, 32
Chromic iron at Port-au-Port, 96, 97
Climate of Newfoundland, 108-111, 150
Coal-fields near Grand Lake, 88, 99; in St. George's Bay, 88, 98, 99
Coast-line of Newfoundland, 157
Cochrane, Sir Thomas, 77
Cod fisheries of Newfoundland, the, 42-48, 115-117
Codroy Valley, 87; gypsum in the, 102
Colleges, 159, 160
Colonies, England and her, 35-40; in the reign of Queen Victoria, 54, 55
Columbus, Christopher, and the discovery of America, 2-5, 11, 13, 15, 191; his reception on returning from, 17-19; landfall of, 21; historians and, 28; the fourth centenary celebration, 34

INDEX. 197

Colville, Lord, 167
Commercial Bank, failure of, in 1894, 141
Commercial crisis of 1894, 141-143
Conception Bay, iron ore in, 94-96
Constabulary, the, 130-133
Copper mines, 75, 79; at Tilt Cove, 89-93; at Bett's Cove, 90, 91
"Council of Higher Education," 160
Cow Head, petroleum found near, 103
Crabb's River, 98
Crisis of 1894, the, 141-143
Crops of 1895, 106
Crown lands, 107

D

Daily News (Newfoundland), 135
Dawson, Dr. S. E., on John Cabot, 24, 25, 33
Dawson, Sir William, 92
Deane, Dr. Charles, on Cabot's landfall, 32, 33
Deer, 155
Department of Fisheries, 116, 120-123
Devonshire, and the cod fishery off Newfoundland, 61-69
"Dog-hood" (seal), the, 178, 181
Doun, Sir Daniel, 58
Dufferin, Lord, 38
Dutch monopoly of herring fisheries, 41

E

Education, 159, 160
Edward VI. pensions Sabastian Cabot, 31
Elementary schools, 159
Elford, Mayor of St. John's, 66
Elizabeth, Queen, laws relating to fishing, 42; "the spacious times of," 49; and Sir H. Gilbert, 51, 54; and Sir Walter Raleigh, 56

Emigration, 82
England, Newfoundland the first colony of, 7; the colonies of, 35-40; and the Icelandic fisheries, 44; and the Newfoundland fisheries, 45-48; first attempt to colonize Newfoundland, 49-54; makes treaties with France, 74; struggle with France in North America, 163-171
Enterprise, the, 135
Evening Herald, 135
Evening Telegram, 135
Executive Council, the, 125
Exploits Bay, 93; valley of, 84, 87

F

Farming in Newfoundland, 105-107
Ferdinand, King, 25; and Columbus, 17, 19; and Sebastian Cabot, 30, 31
Ferryland, Sir G. Calvert's mansion at, 59, 60
Finances of the Colony, 136-143
Fire Department of St. John's, 130-133
Fisheries of Newfoundland, VI., VII.; the French and, 42-45; England and, 45-48, 57-61; "merchant adventurers" and the, 62-69; the staple industry of the people, 112-117
Fishermen in Newfoundland, 161, 162
"Fishing Admirals," government by, 67-70, 73
Fishing era, the, 41, 42
Fiske, on La Cosa's map, 24
Fogs off Newfoundland, 109, 110, 150
Forests in Newfoundland, 108
Fortune Bay, 48; herring fishery at, 121
Fossils at Port-au-Port, 149
Fox, Captain, and Columbus's landfall, 21

o 3

France, population of, 37; and the fishing grounds near Newfoundland, 42–45, 48; fishing vessels of, in 1517, 43; attacks on Newfoundland, 59, 60; treaties with England, 74; and the Bank fishery, 116: struggle with England in North America, 8, 163–171
Fraser, Mr. J. D., 133

G

Galvano on John Cabot's voyages, 26
"Gamewell" fire-alarm telegraph system, 133
Gander Valley, 88
Geological survey by Mr. A. Murray, 79, 101, 105
Germany, population of, 37
Gilbert, Sir Humphrey, and Newfoundland, 49–54, 56
Gold-bearing quartz reef at Cape Broyle, 100, 101
Gomara on Sir John Cabot's voyages, 26, 27
Government in Newfoundland, 124–130; by "Fishing Admirals," 67–70, 73
Governor, the, of Newfoundland, 125, 126; the first, *see* Osborne, Captain
Grand Lake, coal-field near, 88, 99
Granite in Newfoundland, 102
Great Banks, cod fisheries on the, 115, 116, 123; seals on the, 179
Green, J. R., the historian, on Sir Humphrey Gilbert, 49; on John Cabot, 190
Greenland seal, the, 178
Grenfell, Dr., 194
Gulf Stream, the, 113, 173–176
Guy, John, and the Newfoundland fisheries, 57, 58
Gypsum, in Bay St. George, 102

H

Hakluyt, records of, 14, 21
Halifax, archbishop of, on Newfoundland, 151, 152
Halifax Asbestos Company, 97
Harbour Grace, railway to, 83, 84; district court in, 130; constabulary at, 131
Harbour Grace Standard, 135
Harbours of Newfoundland, 88
Harp seal, the, 177, 178, 188
Harrisse (historian) on Sebastian Cabot, 27, 29, 31; and Cabot's landfall, 32
Harvey, Mr. A. W., 81
Henry VII. and John Cabot, 16, 17, 20, 25, 29
Henry VIII., letter of John Rut to, 44
Herring fishery, the, 120, 121; at Bay of Islands, 88
Hind, Professor, 114
Holland, herring trade of, 41
Homestead Law, 107, 108
Hood seal, the, 177, 178
Hopwood, Mr. F. J. S., 194
Hore, Robert, attempts to form a colony in Newfoundland, 1536, 44
House of Assembly, the, 125–127
Howe, Commander Curzon, 132
Howley, Mr. J. P., 90, 98, 99
Hudson's Strait, reached by Sebastian Cabot, 30
Humber River, 99; valley of, 84, 87
Humboldt, and Columbus's landfall, 21
Huntsman, sailing vessel, loss of, 186
Hyatt, Professor, on Newfoundland, 148, 149

I

Ice-fields, the perils of the, 185–187
Ice-hunters of Newfoundland, 181
Icelandic fisheries, England and, 44

INDEX. 199

Imperial Federation, 36
Ingornachois Bay, fossils at, 149
Iron mine, near St. John's, 75, 90, 93, 94; near Grand Lake, 88
Iron ore in Newfoundland, 94-97
Irving, and Columbus's landfall, 21
Isabella, Queen, and Columbus, 17
Island Cove, 96
Italy, growing population of, 38

J

James I., 57; and Captain Whitbourne's book on Newfoundland, 59
Johnson, Matthey & Co., 100
Judicature, 130
Jukes, Professor J. B., 98

K

Kennedy, Captain, "Sporting Notes on Newfoundland," 150, 151
Kirke, Sir David, 60

L

Labrador, said to be Cabot's landfall, 22, 23; coasted by Cabot, 26-30; population of, 157; seals off the coast of, 179; current, 113, 114, 175, 176; cod fisheries off the coast of, 116, 123; supreme court of, 130; branch of the Mission to Deep Sea Fishermen at, 194
La Cosa, Juan de, map of 24, 25, 33
La Manche, lead ore discovered at, 101, 102
Land, value of, for agricultural purposes, 107
Land grants to railway contractor, 84-87
Lead ore, discovered at La Manche, 101, 102; at Port-au-Port, 102
Legislative Council, the 125-127
Lighthouses, 134

Little, Mr. J. J., 81
Little Bay, mine at, 90
Live stock, value of, in 1891, 106
Lobster fishery, 122, 123, 169
Logan, Sir William, 91 n.
Lords, House of, delegation to the, 170
Lumbering, 75, 88, 105
Lumber trade, the, 108

M

Mackay, Mr. A. M., 81
McCowen, Mr. J. R. 131-133
McKay, Mr. Smith; and copper mine at Tilt Cove, 89-92
Maps, Toscanelli's, 13, 14; La Cosa's 24; Sebastian Cabot's, 25
Marble beds, Bay of Islands, 88, 102
Markham, Sir C. R.; on John Cabot, 8, 9, 25, 32
Martyr, Peter, on John Cabot's voyages, 26
Matthew, the, John Cabot's vessel, 1-7, 11-16
Max Müller, Professor, 34
"Merchants Adventurers," and the Newfoundland cod fishery, 62-69, 73
Merchants' Bank of Halifax, 135
Middle Cove, 148
Milan, historic documents in the State Archives of, 19-21
Miquelon, island of, ceded to France, 48, 74, 167-169
Mission to Deep Sea Fishermen. Labrador branch of, 194
Monson, Sir William, and the Newfoundland fisheries, 45
Montreal, 164
Mountain ranges, 149
Municipal tax in St. John's, 137
Murray, Mr. Alexander, geological survey by, 79, 91 n, 101
Murray, Sir Herbert, 132

INDEX

N

Nansen, Dr., 35
Navarelte, and Columbus's landfall, 21
Neptune, s.s., 119, 182
Newfoundland, John Cabot discovers the island in the *Matthew*, 1-7, 11-16, 18-20, 32, 33, 40; England and, 39, 40; the French and the fishing grounds near, 42-44; England and the fisheries of, 45-48; Sir Humphrey Gilbert's first attempt to colonize, 49-54; other attempts to colonize, 57-61; population of, in various years, 60; "Merchant Adventurers" and the fisheries of, 62-69; government by "Fishing Admirals" in, 67-70, 73; the first Governor of, 70; record of progress in the Queen's reign, 75, 76; a mere fishing station, 77; roads in, 78; geological survey of 79; railways constructed in, 79-88; as a health resort, 86, 87; harbours of, 88; prospecting in, 89, 90; copper mining in, 90, 91; iron ore in, 94-97; coal-fields of, 98-100; gold, silver, and gypsum found in, 100-102; discovery of petroleum in, 103; agriculture and farming in, 104-107; forests of, 108; climate of, 108-111; the fisheries the staple industry of the people of, 112-117; cod fisheries of, 115-117; the seal fishery, 117-120; the herring fishery, 120, 121; the salmon fishery, 121, 122; the lobster fishery, 122, 123; government of, 124-130; Supreme Court of, 130; constabulary and fire department, 130-133; population of, 127, 157-159; post-office, 133, 134; lighthouses, 134; banks 135; the newspaper press of, 135; finances of, 136-143; a lightly taxed country, 137; trade and commerce of, in 1896, 142, 143; scenery of, 144-155; as a health resort, 146; Captain Kennedy on the climate of, 150, 151; sport in, 155; geographical position of, 156; its bays and coastline, 157; education in, 159, 160; religious denominations in, 160; classes in, 161, 162; struggle of England and France over, 165-171; account of the great seal hunt in, 173-188; fourth centenary celebration in, 193
Newfoundland Mineral Syndicate, 97
Newspaper press, the, of Newfoundland, 135
Nicholl, and Sebastian Cabot, 26
Nicholls, Mr. J. F.; memoir of Sebastian Cabot, 9, 10, 26
Normandy, fishermen of, off Newfoundland, 42, 44
North, Cape, 25; cliffs of, 149
North America, John Cabot the real discoverer of, 6, 7, 26, 33; struggle of England and France in, 163-171
North American waters, catch of cod in, 116, 117
Norway, scenery of Newfoundland equal to that of, 145-155; cod fisheries of, 115
Notre Dame Bay, 89
Nova Scotia Steel Company, 95

O

Oil extracted from the blubber of seals, 119, 179
Osborne, Captain Henry, first Governor of Newfoundland, 70

P

Pacific Ocean, the, 4, 5
Palos, port of, Columbus at, 17, 19
Paper Pulp Act, 108
Paris, Treaty of, 167
Pasqualigo, Lorenzo, on John Cabot, 5, 19, 20, 23

INDEX. 201

Pelts (seal-skins), 118, 183, 184
People, the, 135
Petroleum, 75; near Cow Head, 103
Petty Harbour, 148
Pilley's Island, iron pyrites mine on, 75, 90, 93–94
Placentia, Basque tombstone found in, 43; road to, from St. John's, 78; railway to, 84; the French in, 165
Placentia Bay, 145; silver mine at, 102; herring fishery at, 121
Polo, Marco, 14
Population of the island, 157–159
Port-au-Basques (harbour), 43; railway to, 84, 86, 147
Port au-Port, 98; chromic iron at, 96, 97; lead ore found at, 102; fossils at, 149
Post-Office, 133, 134
Portuguese fishermen off Newfoundland, 43, 44
Prima Vista, spot so named by John Cabot, 15
Privy Purse accounts, 1497, at the British Museum, 17
Protestants in Newfoundland, 128
Puebla, Spanish envoy, 21
Public debt of the Colony, 137–140

Q

Quebec, 164, 166

R

"Ragged-jackets" (seals), 185
Railways in Newfoundland, 75, 79–88, 138
Raleigh, Sir Walter, and the Newfoundland fisheries, 45; and Sir Humphrey Gilbert, 50, 51; Colony of Virginia, 56, 57
Ramusio, on John Cabot's voyages, 26, 27
Ray, Cape, 43, 103, 168
Reeks, Mr., articles on petroleum in the *Zoologist*, 103

Reid, Mr. Robert G., railway contractor, 84-88, 103, 107
Religious denominations in Newfoundland, 160
Representative government, 125–127
Retrenchment policy in Newfoundland, 140–143
Retriever, s.s., loss of, 186
Revenue of Newfoundland, 136–143
Roads in Newfoundland, 77, 78
Robinson's Brook, coal near, 98, 99
Rose Blanche, village, 148
Royal Gazette, 135
Royal Society of Canada, papers read before, by Dr. S. E. Dawson, 24, 25; and the Cabot centenary, 193
Russia, growing population of, 38
Rut, John, letter to Henry VIII., 44

S

St. George's Bay, 80, 84, 149; valley of, 87; coalfield in, 88, 98, 99; iron ore near, 96; gypsum at, 102; forests round, 108; herring fishery at, 121
St. John's, ships in the harbour of, 1527, 44; Sir H. Gilbert arrives at, 51, 52; population of, in 1834, 72; iron mine near, 75; road to Placentia, 78; district court in, 130; the constabulary and fire department of, 130–133; post office in, 133–134; municipal tax in, 137; dry dock at, 138; schools in, 159, 160; captured by the French in 1708, 165; and in 1762, 166
St. John's Cape, 168
St. John's Island, 149
St. Lawrence, French and English in the region of, 47; Newfoundland the key of the, 156
St. Paul's Inlet, petroleum found near, 103

St. Pierre, island of, ceded to France, 48, 74, 116, 165-169
Salisbury, Lord, on Newfoundland, 74
Salmon fishery, 121, 122
Sandford, Mr., 80
Savings Bank, 135; run on the, 141, 142
Scenery in Newfoundland, 145-155
Scholarship, new, founded, 160
Seal fishery, the, 117-120
Seal-hunt of Newfoundland, account of the, 173-188
Seal hunters, the hardy, 176, 181
Settlers, early, in Newfoundland, the "merchant adventurers" and, 64-69
Shea, Sir Ambrose, 81
Signal Hill, 167
"Silver Cliff Mine," Placentia Bay, 102
Skins of seals, price of, 119
Snowstorms, 110, 186-187
Soncino, Raimondo di, on John Cabot, 20, 21, 23
Southampton, Earl of, 58
Spain and America, 8, 48; and Columbus, 17-19; Sebastian Cabot transfers his services to, 30, 31; fishermen from, off Newfoundland, 43, 48
Spear, Cape, 156
Sport in Newfoundland, 155
Sportsmen and Newfoundland, 86
Square flipper seal, the, 177, 178
Squirrel, the, Sir H. Gilbert's vessel, 52
Steam ferry between Newfoundland and Canada, 75
Stow's Chronicle and John Cabot's second voyage, 26
Supreme Court, the, 130
Sydney, Cape Breton, 86, 147

T

Tarducci, Francesco, on Cabot's landfall, 33; his memoir of the Cabots', 191-192

Taxation in the Colony, 137
Thirkill, Lancelot, 9
Thorburn, Sir Robert, 84
Thorne, Robert, letter of, in 1527, 44
Thunderstorms, 111
Tilt Cove, copper mine at, 79, 89, 90, 92
Times, the, on Newfoundland, 152-154
Topsail, 148
Toscanelli's map of the world, 13, 14
Trade Review, the, 135
Treaty shore, the French and, 169, 170
Trinity Bay, 145
Trinity Record, the, 135
Truck system, the, 143
Twillingate Sun, the, 135

U

Union Bank, failure of, in 1894, 141
United States fisheries, value of, 113
Utrecht, Treaty of, and the Island of Newfoundland, 165-167

V

Vegetation, 110
Versailles, Treaty of, 167, 169
Vessels engaged in cod fisheries, 1891, 116
Victoria, Queen, the Colonies in the reign of, v., vi., 54, 55, 171; Newfoundland's record of progress in the reign of, vi., vii., 75, 76; and the Labrador branch of the Mission to Deep Sea Fishermen, 194
Virginia, Sir Walter Raleigh founds the Colony of, 56, 57
Voting by ballot, 126, 128

W

Watling Island, Columbus's landing place, 21
Whitbourne, Captain Richard, 61; book on Newfoundland, 58, 59
Whitbourne, town of, 59
"White-coats" (seals), 118, 179, 180, 182, 183, 185
Whiteway, Sir William, constructs railways in the Colony, 80-88; heads a delegation to the House of Lords, 170
William III., statute of (government by "Fishing Admirals"), 67-70
Willoughby, Sir Percival, 58
Windsor Lake, s.s., 186, 187
Winter in Newfoundland, 110
Wolf, s.s., 186, 187
Wolfe, General, 47

Z

Zoologist, Mr. Reek's articles on petroleum in, 103

THE END.

LONDON: PRINTED BY WILLIAM CLOWES AND SONS, LIMITED,
STAMFORD STREET AND CHARING CROSS.

www.ingramcontent.com/pod-product-compliance
Lightning Source LLC
Chambersburg PA
CBHW031735230426
43669CB00007B/349